STENCILLING

CAMDEN HOUSE

STENCILLING

A HARROWSMITH GUIDE

SANDRA BUCKINGHAM

 © Copyright 1989 Sandra L. Buckingham

Reprinted: 1990; 1991; 1993; 1995

Canadian Cataloguing in Publication Data

Buckingham, Sandra Lynn, 1944–
    Stencilling: a Harrowsmith guide

ISBN 0-920656-09-9 (pbk.)   0-920656-92-7 (bound)

1. Stencil work.   I. Title.

TT270.B82   1989   745.7'3   C89-094556-X

Published by Camden House Publishing
(a division of Telemedia Communications Inc.)

Camden House Publishing, Suite 100, 25 Sheppard Avenue West, North York, Ontario M2N 6S7

Camden House Publishing, Box 766, Buffalo, New York 14240-0766

Printed and distributed under exclusive licence from Telemedia Communications Inc. by Firefly Books,
250 Sparks Avenue, Willowdale, Ontario, Canada M2H 2S4

Firefly Books (U.S.) Inc., P.O. Box 1338, Ellicott Station, Buffalo, New York 14205

Design by
Linda J. Menyes

Colour separations by
Hadwen Graphics
Ottawa, Ontario

Printed and bound in Canada by
D.W. Friesen & Sons
Altona, Manitoba

Printed on acid-free paper

ACKNOWLEDGEMENTS

To Daniel and William, for their help, their hindrance, their enthusiasm and inspiration and, above all, their patience.

No book is created by its author alone, and this book is no exception. Having no formal historical training, I depended on the expertise of others to guide me through our decorative past. The Historical Research Division of Parks Canada was particularly helpful, especially historians Wayne Grainger, Felicity Leung and Victoria Baker. Cora Greenaway graciously shared the results of her many years of searching out historical decoration in Nova Scotia. Nigel Hutchins, Stuart Stark and Janet Bingham generously helped me find examples of historical stencilling. I also relied heavily on the resources of the Vancouver Public Libraries, the Provincial Archives of British Columbia, the Vancouver City Archives, the Canadian Museum for Textiles and the Fine Arts Library of the University of British Columbia, whose many 19th- and early-20th-century volumes gave me a fascinating look at the decorative practices of the day. The archival series of Dover Publications proved an especially valuable source of historical designs.

I want to thank Barbara Koroluk for getting me started, John Andrews and Jane Rainford for giving me the chance to teach, Claudette Martin and Jim Ziegler for finding me a publisher, Helen Hahn for her penmanship and Robin Richardson for his carpentry. I also thank Robert Duis for his photography.

Special thanks are due to the editors who helped shape this book. Merilyn Mohr guided my efforts and moulded and polished the text. Linda Menyes worked her visual magic on the design and layout of the book, and together with photographer Ernie Sparks, she turned my stencilling efforts into wonderful photographs. Assistant editor Mary Patton, Catherine DeLury and Patricia Denard-Hinch expertly brought the text to its final form. Special thanks to friends, neighbours, relatives and local businesses that lent us props for the pictures.

Finally, thanks to my husband and those friends and relatives who kept our children entertained whenever I had to meet the various deadlines in the production of the book.

CONTENTS

INTRODUCTION

I first became aware of painted wall decoration in 1974, when my husband and I spent a year working in Schloss Laxenburg, an Austrian castle south of Vienna. The schloss, with its hundreds of acres of parkland containing an artificial lake, a small mediaeval castle, a jousting field and a 19th-century re-creation of a Gothic castle, once belonged to the imperial Hapsburg family, who used it as a sort of summer cottage. After World War II, the buildings were in ruins, but in the early 1970s, the Austrian government began to restore them as quarters for a new East-West cooperative scientific venture.

When we joined the organization, only a few rooms of the schloss had been restored to their original glory. Others were in various stages of completion, and the rest of the place was still rubble. Walking from our offices to the library was like flipping through the pages of a manual on historical restoration. We passed by bombed-out rooms filled with collapsed timbers and broken rock, through freshly plastered corridors and over conduits laid under marble floors to carry such modern

baby's room. And with stripes, no less, because that way, I would not have to line up repeats in the pattern. It was not that I didn't want to carry out my noble decorative intentions; it was just that I didn't know how, and I was too intimidated to think that I, without any formal artistic training, could actually figure out what to do. I also suffered from what I call blank-page-itis, the paralysis that occurs whenever I am faced with a blank page, a blank canvas or a blank wall. From a literary perspective, I am at my best when stuck behind the wheel of the car taxiing the kids to school, swim club or soccer practice—times when there is absolutely no opportunity to put thoughts on paper. Artistically, it is the same thing. I will dream up beautiful designs on the margins of the Yellow Pages of the telephone directory while a clerk has me on indefinite hold, or doodle creatively on the back of an envelope while waiting for a boring meeting to end. But give me a paintbrush and a blank wall, and I can't move.

Part of what kept me from pouring my mental images onto walls was the fear of making a mistake. Then one day, without knowing exactly what stencilling really was, I signed up for a two-hour course on the subject. I stencilled two teddy bears and a heart on a piece of fabric and was promptly hooked. Stencilling, I discovered, is simply the use of a template to make a painted image of something—a method that makes creativity almost idiot-proof. I could plan everything ahead of time, make drafts and corrections in pencil, then when the design was just

amenities as electrical wiring, telephone lines and plumbing.

The rooms that were nearing completion took our breath away. Rich brocade covered the walls, elaborate mouldings surrounded doors and windows, parquet floors shone underfoot, and enormous portraits of the imperial family gazed down from their gold-encrusted frames. Sometimes, we would watch a workman—we called them workmen, but they were obviously highly skilled craftsmen—apply gold leaf to the trimmings of a room. During one of our stays in Austria, I had an office high in

the belvedere, an enclosed lookout above the roof of the schloss, in part of what used to be the nursery for the Empress Maria Theresa's children. The walls were decorated with painted latticework, arbours and mountainscapes, the overall effect of which was so delightful that I decided if I ever had children, I would create a similarly imaginative space for them. I was further inspired by the 18th-century ceiling painting in what is now the dining room—once the salon of Archduchess Marie Christine. Every Wednesday evening, an American scientist and I would

deliver ourselves to this room and stumblingly attempt to keep up with the Laxenburg Folk Dancing Club, which used the premises for its weekly practices. I still have vivid memories of gazing up at the bucolic cheerfulness of the country scenes encircling the ceiling as I tried to catch my breath between polkas and waltzes.

The memory of that decorative artistry stayed with me long after we returned to Canada, and when I eventually did have children, it should have inspired a nursery brimming with fantasy. Instead, I wallpapered the

the way I wanted it, I could cut a stencil and use it as a template to paint the image. As long as I used a stencil, the shape of the image would be exactly as planned, and unless I made some gross error when applying the paint, so would the colour and shading.

With the enthusiasm of the recently converted, I threw myself into this new hobby, reading everything I could find, experimenting with different materials and, yes, transforming the walls of our house. Our house is no Austrian schloss, however; it is more like a constantly evolving work-in-progress than a finished *objet d'art*, because as soon as I complete a project, I usually think of some way to make it better. As a result, most of our interior decoration is more or less temporary. If any of it happens to look complete, it is only because the new ideas for that wall have not quite jelled yet. The only permanent fixtures around the house are cans of paint, brushes drying on the windowsill and scraps of Mylar on the floor.

When I first started stencilling a decade ago, almost no one in Vancouver knew what it was. At least one of my friends thought it had something to do with the old-fashioned copying machines that once inhabited every school office. However, in the United States, particularly in the east, it had already become a popular hobby, and it was making inroads into those parts of Canada close to New England. The current revival of decorative stencilling is largely a result of renewed interest in early-19th-century North American decorative arts. Many of the stencil books that have appeared since place particular emphasis on the examples found in New England, reinforcing, in North America, an association of the craft with that part of the United States and with that particular 19th-century rural style.

Stencilling is a tool, however, not a style. The use of templates to create patterns is an age-old technique, and historical examples can be found in many cultures. Images were stencilled on bark cloth in Fiji, on the walls of Buddhist monasteries in China, on early Japanese textiles, on 15th-century European playing cards and on Victorian wallpapers. Very early examples of stencilled interior decoration in

the last 200 years, wallpaper and stencilled decoration have often alternated in popularity, with the nod going to whichever was cheaper—except in the case of the very rich, who could afford to choose according to personal preference. After World War I, stencilling gradually died out, until the American bicentennial revived popular interest in earlier decorating techniques.

Today, after many decades of neglect, stencilling is once again widely used in home decoration, at both the professional and the do-it-yourself levels—on walls, floors, furniture and textiles, not to mention the host of knick-knacks that adorn "country" interiors. Stencilling provides a wonderfully versatile alternative to wallpaper, especially in those older homes where vertical walls and right-angled corners are unknown. It allows you to achieve just the amount of pattern you want, from plain walls with a simple border to a seamless simulation of wallpaper. And stencilled walls have a character and uniqueness about them that wallpaper does not impart. The scope of stencilling throughout the house is practically limitless. You can embellish a tablecloth with a border patterned after the design on your china or use a motif from a carpet to stencil cushions, curtains or window borders. Almost any type of surface can be stencilled, as long as it is not slippery, highly glossy or waxed.

Stencilling is a particularly versatile craft and one that demands neither a great deal of artistic ability nor long and arduous training, especially given modern paints and transparent stencil material. Once you learn

Europe are few and far between, however; they seem to be confined to churches and important public buildings.

Perhaps the greatest stimulus to decorative wall painting was the invention of the chimney in the 13th century. To prevent drafts, the chimney hood was sealed with plaster, a layer of which was eventually applied to walls all the way around the room. The smooth white walls must have invited decoration; sometimes painted to resemble brick or stone, they gradually took on more decorative motifs, often coats of arms and symbols

of heraldry, a task for which the stencil was ideally suited. In England, there are enough surviving examples of stencilled decoration that we know it was used in secular buildings from the 15th century on and in mediaeval churches from even earlier times. In the 17th, 18th and 19th centuries, hand-stencilled wallpaper was produced, but it was gradually replaced by cheaper, factory-printed wall coverings. By the 18th and 19th centuries, the stencil was acknowledged as a humble decorative tool and was probably used fairly commonly to decorate the

plain distempered walls of modest cottages.

As stencilling was so widespread in Europe, particularly in England, it is not surprising that early immigrants to North America brought the technique with them. Since then, stencilling has gone through periods of popularity and disuse and through many decorative styles, from the crudely primitive to the very elegant. It has usually been employed as a substitute for wallpaper, and as such, no matter what the style, it is usually applied in borders, friezes and vertical stripes. Throughout a few basic techniques, you will be amazed at how creative you can be, and you will discover the special thrill of lifting a stencil to reveal the first print of a new pattern.

The instructional part of this book is based on the stencilling classes that I have been teaching in Vancouver, British Columbia, for the past several years. It is designed to teach the absolute beginner everything he or she needs to learn to become an accomplished stenciller, but many of the sections will also interest those who are already skilled in the craft. Chapter One covers basic instructions: what sort of materials to use, how to cut a stencil, how to apply the paint, how to deal with mistakes. It also discusses what you need to do before you put the first stencil to wall or floor. The next chapter contains step-by-step exercises, each building on the one before to produce a repertoire of stencilling skills and techniques. This is followed by a chapter of specific projects, starting with simple designs for wrapping paper and greeting cards and ending with an intricately stencilled floor. Then, because children's rooms are so much fun to decorate with the help of stencils, there is a chapter devoted solely to that. The final pages of the book focus on design: a discussion of the 19th- and 20th-century decorative styles used in Canada is followed by a design glossary containing dozens of inspiring patterns from all periods. The book closes with a source list of materials to help you get started and some suggested reading for those who become as hooked on the art of stencilling as I am.

IN HER OWN KITCHEN, THE AUTHOR, FACING PAGE, STENCILLED A LATTICED FRIEZE AT THE TOP OF HER KITCHEN WALL, THE DESIGN MIMICKING WOODEN LATTICEWORK THAT ENCLOSES A GAZEBO OUTSIDE THE KITCHEN WINDOW. SHE USED A SECOND STENCIL, RANDOMLY POSITIONED, TO PAINT WISTERIA DANGLING THROUGH THE SPACES. BORDERS CAN ALSO BE USED IN THE MIDDLE OF A WALL, ABOVE WAINSCOTTING AND CHAIR RAILS, TO DECORATE AND DEFINE THE TRANSITION. YOU CAN PERSONALIZE A SERPENTINE LEAF BORDER BY ADDING, FOR EXAMPLE, GOLDEN BERRIES, ABOVE, OR FLORAL MOTIES, LEFT.

CHAPTER ONE

BASIC TECHNIQUES

There is more than one right way to stencil and more than one way to go wrong. If you have never stencilled before, following proven methods will certainly save you a lot of frustration. But once you have the hang of it, feel free to experiment and to invent your own variations and shortcuts. In this chapter, I describe what works best for me, but there are other ways that work too. In fact, I have a motto that I like to pass on to my classes: "If it works, it's the right way."

Boiled down to its essentials, stencilling is nothing more than cutting a shaped hole in some material and using the cutout as a template for applying colour. This chapter describes how to make the cutout and how to apply the colour, but to start with, there are some suggestions about the sorts of materials to use. Read through the chapter to get an overview of what you are getting yourself into, then, following the instructions for cutting and painting, try the first few exercises in Chapter Two.

EQUIPMENT

You don't need a lot of expensive equipment to learn to stencil. The biggest financial outlay will be for paint and a few good brushes, but even they will cost far less than the wallpaper required to cover a small room. The main things you need are: something to cut a stencil out of, something to cut it with, some paint and something to put the paint on with. Let's go through those in order.

STENCIL MATERIAL

Almost any flat material that can be cut and is impervious to paint can be used for stencils. In Fiji, stencillers once used banana leaves; nowadays, as in most of the South Pacific, they use old X-ray film. The Japanese use a tough paper made of mulberry fibre and persimmon juice. Early American painters used metal, leather or shellacked paper for their stencils. You can use cardboard, heavy paper, foil or Mactac. I once used an old vinyl tablecloth. However, the process is much easier if the stencil is transparent: you can see through it to line it up with the part of the design that has already been painted.

I prefer 5-mil clear Mylar. Polyester film is its generic name, and it is available at stores selling art and craft supplies. Material that is thicker is too hard to cut, and thinner film is not quite rigid enough. Mylar is very durable, easy to clean and completely transparent, which makes cutting and stencilling easier. Buy it in flat sheets rather than cut from a roll, because the curl can be difficult to eliminate. I don't like vinyl, which I find too floppy, especially in warm weather. But I do use Mactac—thin vinyl with an adhesive backing—for odd-shaped surfaces, for the corners of rooms and for tiny, finicky stencils because it is so easy to cut and hold in place. Mactac is not appropriate for designs with large cutouts, however, because it is so thin. Some books recommend acetate for stencils, but I never use it, as it tears too easily. Acetate looks very much like Mylar, so be sure to ask

16

what the material is before you buy. If you cannot find any polyester film, try using stencil board, a heavy paper stock often used for commercial letter stencils. Although it is opaque, it is inexpensive, easy to cut and very tough. I often use it for very large stencils where strength is important.

CUTTING TOOLS

The most important factor in cutting a good stencil is a sharp blade. Utility and X-acto knives both work well, although my students seem to have better luck with the latter because the blade is narrower and mounted more firmly. Some utility knives have blades that wobble from side to side, making accurate cuts difficult. Whichever knife you use, the blades are very sharp, so exercise caution when cutting and never leave them where children can get at them. As it is essential to work with a very sharp edge, it is a good idea to keep extra blades on hand. I got tired of buying replacements, so I switched to stainless steel blades that I resharpen as required with a small sharpening stone.

A self-healing cutting mat, which you can buy at fabric, hobby and graphic-supply stores, makes cutting easier and preserves the edge on the blade, but it is not essential. Any smooth, hard surface a piece of arborite countertop, plate glass, thick cardboard or wood that does not have a pronounced grain—can be used as a stencil-cutting surface. You can even use a stack of newspapers.

If you are nervous about using very sharp knives or if you have trouble cutting accurately with a blade, scissors are a good alternative. Small scissors such as those used for manicures or embroidery are best; be sure that they are comfortable to hold and have sharp, accurate blades.

PAINTS

In theory, you can use almost any kind of paint as long as it is not too runny and you keep the brush quite dry. In practice, however, it is much easier to obtain good results with stencil paints. These are specially formulated to dry very quickly so that you can move the stencil without smudging the design. There are several types of stencil paint available:

• *Fabric paints and dyes* are designed to leave the painted part of the fabric as supple as the unpainted cloth. To make the colour permanent, some kind of heat treatment is usually necessary—several minutes under a hot iron or half an hour in a hot commercial dryer. Fabric paints may not be suitable for all types of fabric, so read the label carefully. They are, however, the best paints to use for paper projects, except in cases where you need an opaque paint to make the stencil visible on a very dark background. In this case, acrylics are preferable. Fabric paints can also be used on walls and wooden objects, although here the paints should be protected with varnish.

• *Japan paints* are concentrated, finely ground pigments in a varnishlike medium that dries instantly. They can be thinned with turpentine if necessary. Japan paints are easy to shade, go on very smoothly and do not build up rapidly on the stencil. I prefer them for hard surfaces such as walls and floors.

• *Acrylic paints* are water-soluble but dry to form a tough skin

on brushes and stencils. This skin is very hard to remove, making cleanup difficult for large projects. Acrylics are not my favourite paints, but I do sometimes use them, especially if I don't want the smell or poison hazard of turpentine. They are more opaque than other paints, so they are particularly useful when you want to stencil on a dark or figured background. When applied to fabrics, they do not require heat treatment for permanence, which eliminates the extra step. They will not bend with the material, but if the fabric is stiff to begin with, as it may be for floor cloths, wall hangings and place mats, an inflexible paint is no disadvantage.

• *Stencil crayons* are oil-based wax crayons that you rub onto the stencil near the cut-out parts; you then work the brush around in the wax and gradually blend the colour into the design area. This method is basically smearproof because the colours are solid rather than liquid, but I find it slow and physically tiring. Mineral spirits or turpentine are used for cleanup.

• *Spray paints* (available in aerosol cans from paint stores) can also be used for stencilling. The colour range is not as great as for other paints, but you can blend and mix colours by applying successive layers of fine spray in different hues.

• *Bronze powders*, finely ground metal alloys, are available in a variety of colours from art-supply stores. Rubbed through stencil cutouts onto an almost dry layer of varnish, they create elegant, glowing images.

PAINT APPLICATORS

Stencil brushes look like shaving brushes—short, fat and blunt-cut across the tip. How flexible the bristles should be depends on the technique used and the surface being stencilled. Stippling requires a very stiff brush, but smooth, circular application works better if the bristles bend a bit. On fabric, you need a stiff brush regardless of the way the paint is applied. For paper, buy a brush that holds its shape well but is not so stiff that it scrapes the surface. Whatever its flexibility, be sure the brush is solidly packed with bristles.

You can buy brushes at graphic-supply stores, fabric stores and tool outlets. They do not have to be specifically labelled as stencilling brushes (cabinetmakers' gluing brushes are excellent). You should have a separate brush for each colour in a project; it is also useful to have a few different sizes. Don't buy a whole collection of brushes at once, though, because you will find that you end up liking some kinds and brands better than others. Start with one or two and get more as you need them. Whenever I travel, I keep an eye out for brushes. One of my favourites is a small, round house-painting brush that I bought for $5 in a rural grocery store.

Brushes aren't the only things you can use to paint a stencil. Sponges work (they give a different texture to the print) and so do airbrushes and spray paints. An airbrush is an expensive investment, however, and as with spray paints, the technique takes time to master. The area to be stencilled must be carefully masked to ensure that none of the fine paint mist goes astray, and you have to wear goggles and a mask to protect your eyes and lungs. I find it difficult to achieve the same control with a spray can that I have with a brush. Furthermore, the paint builds up quickly on the stencil, and unless it is glued to the work surface, the edges of the images will not be very crisp. Some stencillers swear by spray paint, however. If you want to try it, see *The Art of Stencilling* by Lyn Le Grice. For designs with large painted areas, small rollers are faster than brushes, though you will use more paint because of the amount soaked up by the roller. In one of my more improvised improvisations, I stencilled a moon and stars on my son's bedroom wall using cardboard stencils, ordinary interior latex paint and an ordinary, large wall-painting brush. I had to bunch up the bristles in my fist to keep them from getting under the edge of the cardboard. Before long, paint covered my hand and dribbled down my arm. I had to be very careful to avoid smudging because the paint was slow to dry. The final results were pretty good, but I would not recommend the technique. It was weeks before I got all the paint out from under my fingernails.

THERE IS MORE THAN ONE WAY TO APPLY STENCIL PAINT, AND EACH APPLICATOR CREATES A UNIQUE EFFECT. THE BORDER BELOW WAS PAINTED USING A CIRCULAR RUBBING MOTION WITH A BRUSH THAT HAD FLEXIBLE BRISTLES. THE BORDERS ON THE FACING PAGE, TOP TO BOTTOM, WERE STIPPLED WITH A STIFF BRUSH, SPRAY-PAINTED AND COLOURED BY DAUBING PAINT THROUGH A STENCIL WITH A SPONGE. ALL FOUR BORDERS WERE ADAPTED FROM THE GINGERBREAD TRIM ON VICTORIAN HOUSES.

CUTTING STENCILS

THE SIMPLEST WAY TO CUT A STENCIL IS TO TAPE A SHEET OF MYLAR OVER A PHOTOCOPY OF THE DESIGN. CUT ALONG THE OUTLINE, ABOVE, USING YOUR OTHER HAND TO TURN THE MYLAR SLOWLY SO THAT YOU ALWAYS CUT TOWARD YOURSELF. CUT AWAY FROM THE NARROW BRIDGES OR TIES IN A DESIGN, FACING PAGE, DOING THE SMALLEST CUTOUTS FIRST. FOR A SMOOTH CURVE, CUT WITHOUT LIFTING THE KNIFE. FOR CLEAN, SHARP CORNERS, MAKE TWO SEPARATE CUTS FROM OPPOSITE DIRECTIONS, OVERCUTTING THE CORNER A LITTLE ON EACH SIDE.

Stencil cutting is easier than most people think, but it sometimes takes a little practice to become really good at it. All you need is a sharp blade and a good eye. I will describe methods for cutting both transparent and opaque stencils, as well as some alternative techniques in case you have difficulty.

Most stencil books tell you to copy the design onto the stencil material before cutting. I use a different method, one that I find faster and more accurate, but it only works for transparent material. First make a photocopy of the chosen design, then use pencil crayons to indicate the colour of each part. As a general rule,

you will need to cut a separate stencil for each colour. Put the photocopy on the cutting board, or whatever you use to protect the table, and place a sheet of Mylar on top. Make sure it is positioned so that there is a border of an inch or more around the edge of the design. Tape the Mylar to the photocopy but not to the board. Now you are ready to cut.

Holding the knife as you would a pencil, begin cutting along the outline of the design. Keep your other hand firmly on the stencil material, and turn it as you cut so that you are always cutting toward yourself. This provides the best control. If the

blade starts slipping or if your knuckles turn white from pressing too hard, then you need a fresh blade. The cut pieces should pop out easily. If a piece hangs on in one spot, trim it off carefully – don't try to tear it. To get a smooth curve, try to cut without lifting the blade. To cut sharp corners cleanly, make two separate cuts from opposite directions, overcutting the corner a little on each side. In case you slip, always cut away from areas where there is only a narrow bridge or "tie" of stencil material between the cutouts. Do the smallest cutouts first and the largest last. To get a perfectly straight line, use a metal-edged ruler to guide the knife. Make sure you press down very hard on the ruler to keep it from slipping. Before you untape the stencil material from the pattern underneath, mark some placement lines on it so that the stencil will be correctly positioned on whatever it is you are decorating. If you are doing Christmas cards, for example, you might mark the outline of the card edges on the stencil so that you do not have to guess or fiddle with the exact arrangement of the design for each new card.

The technique for cutting opaque stencils is exactly the same, except that you have to transfer the design to the stencil material first. You can use carbon paper to trace the image, or – as I usually do because I am too lazy to trace – you can glue the paper copy of the design to the stencil material with a temporary adhesive spray (available in art-supply stores). I cut through both paper and stencil, then pull off the paper.

If you are unhappy with your

cutting or with the length of time it took you, don't be discouraged. Practice will make you better and faster. Don't throw away an imperfect stencil without printing it—you will be amazed at how good an image it makes. If you have real difficulties, don't give up. Ask yourself the following:

• Is my knife sharp?
• Is the light good enough?
• Is my eyesight good? Or do I need to have it checked? In almost every one of my classes, there are people who don't realize how old their glasses are until they try to cut a stencil.

If you still have trouble, try using small, sharp scissors instead of a blade. In this case, you will have to trace the design onto the stencil material instead of taping a photocopy to it, even if you are using transparent Mylar. Permanent fine-tipped felt marking pens work well for tracing designs on all types of plastic. If you want to master the knife technique, practise cutting designs out of paper, switching to heavier papers as you become more adept and finally graduating to the desired stencil material. If your pattern has fairly small cutouts and thick bridges, try using clear Mactac. It is very easy to cut with a knife, and its adhesiveness compensates somewhat for its flimsiness.

REGISTRATION

Registration is the lining up or positioning of each stencil before painting. One of the easiest ways to position a transparent stencil is to use markings drawn right on the stencil material with a permanent felt pen. If you make a mistake, alcohol will remove the pen marks. Unfortunately, so will turpentine. In other words, every time you clean your stencils, you risk removing the registration marks that you went to so much trouble to put on. To remedy this little problem, I use X-acto knife scratches instead of pen marks. The scratches show up surprisingly well, even better after they have a little paint on them. You will need three different types of registration marks:

• *Guidelines* to position the stencil with respect to features of the surface you're painting; for example, lining up a frieze six inches below the ceiling.

• *Repeat registration marks* to position the stencil with respect to the previous print in the design, as in a repeating floral print.

• *Colour registration marks* to position the second or third stencil with respect to the part of the motif already printed; for example, a red tulip among green leaves.

It is best to put all three types of registration marks on the stencil when you are cutting it out. The original design should have a guideline and repeats drawn on it. Before you untape the Mylar from the drawing, trace the outlines of the repeats in the design with the cutting knife. Scratch a line on the Mylar to indicate the guideline. If the design requires more than one stencil, use the knife to trace the outside edges of the parts

that will be painted with other stencils. You do not need to redraw the whole design, just enough so that you can position the stencil accurately.

Good registration with opaque stencils requires a little more work. Instead of drawing a guideline on the stencil, cut notches in the sides of the stencil that coincide with the guideline on the design. For repeat registration, cut out a small por-

tion of the repeat design—the tip of a leaf, the bottom of a stem, the outer edge of a petal—on either side of the actual stencil cutouts. The same kind of cutouts can be used to make colour registration marks, although it is a good idea to outline them in permanent felt marker so that you will remember to avoid painting through the registration cutouts when you print the stencil.

NOTCHED GUIDELINES AND COLOUR REGISTRATION MARKS CAN BE SEEN ON THE TWO OPAQUE STENCILS ABOVE. THE HORIZONTAL DASHED LINES, FACING PAGE, ARE GUIDELINES. THE DASHED-LINE MOTIF, TOP, IS A REPEAT REGISTRATION MARK, AND THE LEAVES AND STEM WITH A BROKEN OUTLINE, CENTRE, ARE COLOUR REGISTRATION MARKS.

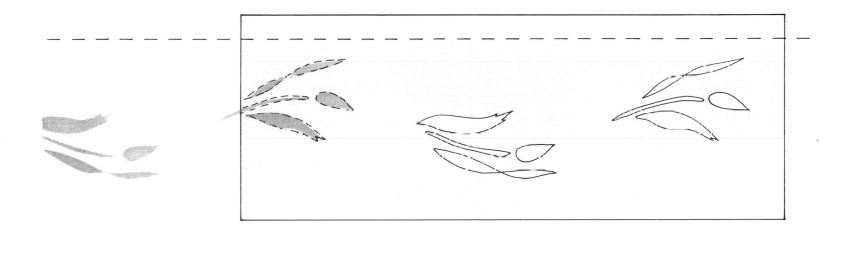

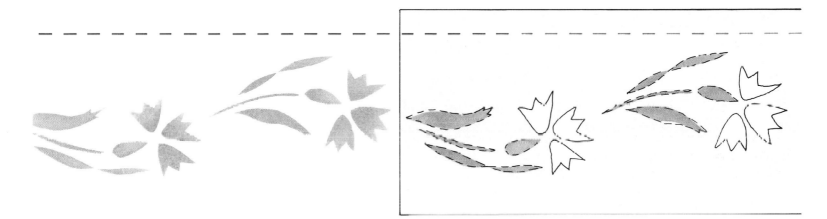

BASIC STENCILLING PROCEDURE

STENCILLING IS BASICALLY A "DRY-BRUSH" TECHNIQUE. HOLDING THE BRUSH LIKE A PENCIL, WITH THE BRISTLES PERPENDICULAR TO THE SURFACE, RUB THE BRUSH IN A CIRCULAR MOVEMENT OR STIPPLE BY MAKING SHORT, DABBING POUNCES. BUILD UP THE COLOUR GRADUALLY, LIFTING THE CORNER OF THE STENCIL TO CHECK ON THE DARKNESS OF THE PRINT. MASTER THE TECHNIQUE BY PRACTISING ON PAPER, AND TRY OUT EACH NEW DESIGN ON SCRAPS OF MATERIAL BEFORE ATTEMPTING THE FINAL STENCIL. THE AUTHOR, ABOVE, STENCILLED THE PATTERN, TOP RIGHT, ONTO TRIANGLES OF FABRIC THAT A MANUFACTURER SEWED TOGETHER TO CREATE AN UMBRELLA, BOTTOM RIGHT.

Do all your practice stencilling on paper. Some types of paper work better than others—watercolour paper is especially good, but it is expensive—so try a few different kinds. You want something cheap to practise on, but you also want something easy to work with. Position the first stencil of your design, and secure it in place with masking tape or low-tack drafting tape. You can also spray temporary adhesive on the back of the stencil. Do not use packing tape, regular Scotch tape or any adhesive that will tear the paper when you pull it off.

Put about half a teaspoon of paint onto a plastic or foam plate; for japan paint, use a glass saucer or a disposable palette sheet. Holding the brush perpendicular to the plate, dip the bristles into the paint. You should have only a tiny dab of paint on the ends of the bristles. Distribute the paint evenly by working the bristles in a circular motion in a clear spot on the plate, being careful not to add any more paint to the brush in the process. Now use the same circular motion on a dry paper towel to remove most of the paint from the brush. I know this sounds ridiculous, but stencilling is essentially a "dry-brush" technique; the most common mistake for a beginner is to have too much paint on the brush, which produces a blotchy or smudged print. Practise a bit on paper, and you will see what I mean. (You will be surprised how little paint is used. One small two-ounce jar of paint will probably be enough to do borders around the kitchen as well as on a tablecloth, aprons and tea towels, with enough left over for a year's supply of Christmas cards.)

You are now ready to print your first stencil. Hold the brush like a pencil, with the bristles perpendicular to the surface about to be painted. There are two ways of applying the paint: one is to use a circular rubbing movement, and the other is to stipple, making short, dabbing pounces with the brush. The major disadvantages of stippling are that it is both tiring and noisy, especially if you're pounding out a wall border—the hollow spaces between wall studs amplify the sound like a drum. Nevertheless, experiment with both methods because they produce different effects. For both, the procedure is the same: start applying the paint around the edges of the stencil cutout first, and then gradually work toward the centre. Of course, if the stencil openings are quite small, you will probably end up colouring the whole design at once.

Don't try to produce a dark print all at once. You will get much better results if you build up the colour gradually by going over it several times. Before you get it too dark, lift up a corner of the stencil and check the print, which will always be darker than it looks with the stencil still in place.

Once you are satisfied with the print of the first stencil, untape it, and using the registration marks as a guide, position and tape the second stencil in place. Paint it, and continue with additional stencils until the first print of the design is complete. You will be amazed at how many imperfections vanish when the stencil is lifted.

Because stencil paint dries so fast, it will soon start drying on the brush. When the prints start looking very faint and dry, you need to dampen the bristles with solvent, but only slightly. Keep a folded paper towel moistened with solvent—water for fabric or acrylic paint, turpentine for japan paint—on a corner of the palette plate. (If the smell of turpentine is bothersome, keep an inverted glass dish over the towel.) Dab the end of the brush onto the paper towel, then work the bristles around on a clean corner of the plate before recharging the brush with paint. If paint starts to accumulate around the edge of the brush, wipe the sides of the bristles with the damp paper towel. Do not immerse the brush in solvent until you have finished painting—it will become too wet for stencilling, and you will have to clean it and let it dry before you can continue. If the paint on the plate starts to dry, add a drop of solvent.

To get a feeling for the different effects you can achieve, practise some prints on scrap paper. Try making some wetter and some drier; try loading the brush with different amounts of paint. You will soon discover what you can get away with.

To help myself stay organized while doing all this, I use one plate-sized surface—a plastic, foam or glass plate or a disposable palette sheet—as a work station for each colour. If I am using two colours, I have a second plate for the other colour. One of the problems with trying to do two colours at once is that sooner or later you will load the brush with the wrong colour of paint. Then, unless you have spares, you have to clean the brush and wait for it to dry.

If I have to move around the room to do a border, I put all the immediate supplies on a cookie tray (with edges) that I drag around after me, carrying everything I need in one motion. The rim of the tray has saved me from a disastrous mess more than once when I stepped down from a ladder in a hurry and landed in a jar of paint.

Don't give up a project in dismay because the prints are not perfect and identical. If you want uniformity, you might as well use wallpaper. There is no point in doing hand-painted decoration if it ends up looking as if it were printed by a machine; it is the minor imperfections and variations that say "hand-painted." Of course, you don't want large smudges or drips of paint trailing from the design, but many small flaws will be unnoticeable when you look at the finished project.

The degree of perfection also depends on the style you are trying to achieve. If you look at photographs of historical houses with stencilled decoration, it is difficult to believe that the same tool—namely a stencil—was used to embellish both a rural 18th-century American cottage and a sumptuous French château. The stencilled prints in the former could be naïve in design and crudely printed, while in the latter, they attain the refinement of their elegant surroundings.

Occasionally you will make mistakes. First, assess the damage. If it is a minor flaw, you can hide it with a potted palm or just let it show, and if anyone dares to say anything, raise an eyebrow and look amused. If the flaw really bothers you, touch up the stencil or the background freehand using a small artist's brush, or position the stencil on top of the image but slightly out of line so that the edge of the cutout encloses the smudge, and restencil that part of the image. If the mistake is fairly major and if you catch it right away, you can simply wipe the paint off with a cloth dampened in solvent. Let the solvent dry completely before restencilling. If the paint is indelible and is on a wall or floor, you can paint over the error with background paint (it will probably take a couple of coats) and then restencil once the background patch is dry.

The basic stencilling procedure described above works for any hard surface—walls, floors, paper. The procedure for stencilling on fabric is different, however, because the cloth is not rigid and tends to move around under the brush and because, once stencilled, the cloth is likely at some point or other to be put through a washing machine, and you don't want the paint to wash off. If you want the painted parts of the fabric to remain supple—as you would if you were stencilling on clothing or table linens—you should use fabric paint or dye; if you are stencilling on a wall hanging, place mats or other fabrics that need not drape, acrylic paint is fine. Some dyes are very liquid and need to be mixed with special thickeners to make them more suitable for stencilling. The only real disadvantage to most fabric paints and dyes is that they need to be heat-treated to make them permanent. As heat treatment usually involves pressing with a hot or medium-hot iron for a certain length of time, you should avoid fabrics such as silk that will not take a hot iron. Always read the instructions on the paint label, because the treatment required varies from brand to brand. It is also a good idea to test your technique beforehand on some scraps of fabric. When you press the cloth, make sure you move the iron around, watching carefully for scorching. Give each scrap a different length of time under the heat, then wash them all and see what happens.

Before you begin stencilling on a fabric, prepare it by washing and ironing to remove the sizing and to preshrink and flatten the fibres. Then fasten it down so that it does not wiggle when you try to move a brush over it. The least you should do is tape it securely to a flat surface, but I get better results by stapling the fabric to a board covered with felt. The felt provides enough friction to keep the body of the fabric still. Now tape the stencil in place, load the paintbrush as usual, and start putting the colour on, working first around the edge of the stencil cutout. With fabric, to be sure that the paint gets right into the fibres and not just onto the surface fuzz, I prefer to use a fairly stiff brush and work it in a circular motion. You can stipple the paint on too, but

make sure you really pound it into the fibres. You should build up the colour gradually, and I find I need more paint on the brush than for hard surfaces because the paint soaks into the cloth instead of sitting on top. Lift a corner of the stencil once in a while to see whether you have enough colour. When finished, let the fabric air dry for a few days, then heat-set according to instructions.

CLEANUP

I didn't mention anything about cleaning up at the beginning of the chapter, but there is no way the subject can be avoided. Have you ever been faced with a particularly difficult cooking pot to clean? Burnt porridge comes to mind. My usual approach is to say that I have to let it soak awhile. What I really mean is that I cannot face the job right now and may never be able to, so I fill the pot with soapy water and let it sit. With luck, when I come back later in the day, it will have miraculously cleaned itself. I have tried this approach with stencils, and it doesn't work. (It doesn't work with porridge either.) Hot soapy water has no effect on dirty stencils unless there is a moving scrub brush in there as well.

Your stencils and brushes will last a long time if you clean them properly immediately after each use, although for simple stencils, it is sometimes easier to cut a new one than to clean the old. I like to do the brushes and the stencils at the same time, first using the brushes to clean the stencils, then giving the brushes an extra cleaning of their own.

For water-based paints such as acrylics, use warm soapy water

and gently clean the stencils on both sides, dislodging the paint with the brush. Clean between the bristles of the stencil brush by working it around on a fingernail brush. Then rinse the brushes and stencils well. Brushes should dry overnight before reuse. Let the stencils dry flat on newspapers or paper towels.

For japan paints, clean the brushes and stencils first with solvent, then with soap and warm water. Lay the dirty stencils on a pile of newspaper topped with paper towels. Wet the brush with solvent and work it around on the stencil (as though you were painting) to loosen and dissolve the paint. Wipe carefully around each cutout with paper towels, then wash with soap and water. The brushes are easier to clean than regular house-painting brushes because there is so much less paint in them. The best technique is to use two or three empty jars or tins, each containing some solvent. Work the bristles around in the first jar; spin the brush handle between your palms to work out the excess (keep the bristles below the edge of the jar, or you will spray yourself with solvent), then repeat in the second jar and, if necessary, in the third. Dry the brushes as much as possible with a paper towel, then wash them with warm water and soap. Rinse well, dry with a rag, and let them dry thoroughly overnight before reusing.

FINISHING

Many of your projects, especially furniture, floors and floor cloths, will look better and last longer with a protective finish. The finish brings out the colours and protects the stencils on surfaces

subjected to hard use. Stencilled walls do not generally require a finish coat unless they are vulnerable to grubby fingerprints or they need the special effect of a gloss finish.

Synthetic varnish (called Varathane or urethane) is generally the best type of finish because it is very durable and easy to apply. The first coat should be thinned slightly with turpentine. Varathane is usually available in flat, satin, semigloss and gloss finishes; pick whichever is appropriate to your project. All of these varnishes have a yellowish tinge to them, so you need to take that into account when planning your colours. It is often worthwhile doing a test beforehand on a piece of scrap wood: apply the base coat, the stencils and the varnish to check on the final hues.

Fairly new to the market is a water-based acrylic varnish; it looks milky in the can but dries perfectly clear with no yellow cast. It is ideal for many projects although it is not durable enough for anything underfoot. Floors need the protection of a real varnish or Varathane.

Although japan paint feels dry to the touch almost immediately, it may take days or weeks to cure completely. In the meantime, if you apply a finish like Varathane, which contains the same solvent as japan paint, the seemingly dry paint will liquefy and bleed into the varnish. As a result, it is wise to wait several days before varnishing over paint that has the same solvent as the finish. Always test a small patch first. If the stencil continues to bleed even after sufficient curing time, apply a coat of shellac before varnishing.

BRONZING

There is another stencilling technique that involves much less cleanup. It is called bronzing and uses metal powder—usually bronze—instead of paint. A dark surface is given a coat of varnish, and when it is not quite dry, a stencil is laid down and the bronze powder is rubbed through it onto the tacky surface with a piece of velvet instead of a brush. I hesitated for years before trying this process, because it looked difficult and I thought it would involve buying a lot of new materials, but I was wrong. Bronzing is less messy than stencilling with paint, and it is just as easy and as much fun. I don't think I have to tell you how wonderful it is to finish stencilling and not have a stack of stencils to scrub and brushes to clean. Another advantage is

that the stencils do not have to be very strong. I like to use heavy tracing paper, which is so easy to cut that I can make very small or intricate designs that would be hard to cut out of Mylar or stencil board.

The only things you need for bronzing that you may not already have around the house are a small piece of velvet, felt or chamois (a patch a few inches square is big enough) and a small jar of bronze powder (it comes in different shades, and you only need a tiny bit). You need a dark surface, not necessarily black, to practise on—a painted scrap of smooth wood or a piece of nonabsorbent coloured paper or cardboard will do. A coat of shellac will make cardboard nonabsorbent.

Although my jar of bronze

powder has no safety precautions printed on the label, common sense dictates wearing a dust mask to avoid breathing the extremely fine powder. Close-fitting rubber gloves will protect your skin. After you dole out the small amount of powder needed for a project, refasten the lid securely. I once knocked over an open jar, and it was almost impossible to clean up the spilled powder, so tenaciously did it cling to every surface it touched.

The first step is to brush a thin, smooth coat of semigloss or gloss varnish over the entire practice surface and let it dry to the tacky stage: no longer wet to the touch but offering very slight resistance when you remove your finger. If the varnish is too wet, the velvet will become sticky and collect blobs of powder. Experiment to find just the right stage; I suspect it will be quite a bit drier than you thought. The velvet should run smoothly over it. On my first attempt, I thought I would be clever and use acrylic varnish so that I would not have to wait hours for it to dry and would also be able to wash out the varnishing brush under the tap. But acrylic varnishes dry too quickly, and by the time I had finished one or two leaves of my border, the surface was no longer tacky enough for the powder to adhere. Not only that, but the varnish also dried with brush marks that showed up through the bronze powder, because not as much powder adhered where the varnish was drier. You need a fairly slow-drying varnish and one that coats the surface very smoothly without brush marks.

Now comes the fun part. Put a little powder into a saucer. Position the stencil on the varnished surface—you don't have to tape it, because the surface is tacky. Tape strips of paper to the perimeter of the stencil so that the rest of the varnished surface is well protected from stray bits of powder.

Wrap the velvet around your index finger so that it stretches smoothly across the tip (I hold it in place with a piece of masking tape). Pick up a small amount of powder on the velvet, then rub your finger around on a piece of paper or cloth to distribute the powder evenly and get rid of any excess. Then, gently rub the powder into the tacky surface with a sort of polishing motion. Work the brightest parts of the stencil design first. Very small cutouts will be solidly coloured with the powder, but for large cutouts, the powder should be shaded, usually stronger on the outside and fading to nothing in the centre. To recharge the velvet, pick up powder first from the paper, where it will be less thick than on the saucer. You may find your finger too big for delicate shading in small cutouts. In this case, use a "bob" to apply the powder. You can fashion a bob by folding a square of velvet over the end of a cotton swab and tying it with thread or dental floss. When you have applied the bronze powder to your satisfaction, make sure that there are no loose grains sitting on the stencil or the surface being decorated, because as soon as you lift the stencil, those little grains will find their way to some nice clean spot on the background and stick themselves there.

If the varnish gets too dry before you have finished, or if you are interrupted before finishing the entire surface, leave everything for at least 24 hours, then revarnish and continue stencilling. If you try to revarnish the same day, the stencilled bronze will be picked up (and moved around) by the varnish brush.

I know I implied that there is no cleanup involved, but there is a little bit. When you are finished for the day, wipe both sides of the stencil with solvent to clean off all traces of bronze.

When you are no longer practising but are beginning a real bronze-stencilling project, start by covering the surface to be decorated with flat, eggshell or satin paint in a rich, dark colour. Apply as many coats as you think necessary. Let this background dry completely, sand it smooth, then, to give yourself some insurance in case you need to correct a mistake, give the surface a coat of semigloss varnish. When dry, rub it lightly with No. 0000 steel wool, wipe it with a rag moistened with paint thinner and go over it with a tack cloth (available in paint stores). Now apply a second coat of varnish, let it dry until tacky and stencil as before. When you have completed all the stencilling, let it dry for at least 24 hours, after which you can wash the surface gently with soapy water to remove any unwanted powder. Finally, varnish yet again for protection.

There are some variations on this basic theme—you can, for example, use powders of different colours and float colour on top of them. These techniques are discussed on page 50, after the preliminary exercises.

BRONZING IS BEST APPLIED TO A DARK BACKGROUND WITH A SMALL PIECE OF VELVET OR CHAMOIS WRAPPED AROUND THE INDEX FINGER, FACING PAGE. ONE OF THE SECRETS TO CREATING FLAWLESS BRONZED STENCILS LIKE THE ROUND JEWELLERY BOX, ABOVE AND LEFT, IS TO WASH THE SURFACE LIGHTLY BEFORE APPLYING THE FINAL COAT OF VARNISH. THIS WILL REMOVE ANY POWDER THAT IS NOT SECURELY STUCK ON. MORE STUBBORN STRAY BITS OF METAL POWDER MAY BE REMOVED BY GENTLE POLISHING WITH VERY FINE SANDPAPER OR BY CAREFUL WIPING WITH A COTTON SWAB DAMPENED WITH SOLVENT.

BORDERS

One way or another, most stencilling projects involve borders, so it is worthwhile making some general remarks about their application. With a simple border, once you have laid down a guideline that ensures it will be straight, you just start stencilling at one end and keep going until you reach the other end or arrive back where you started. You might fudge the spacing a bit in an ad hoc fashion as you go so that you don't end with half a leaf, but it is nothing to worry about. Minor changes in spacing will not be noticed.

This is not the case with borders that have more obvious repeats, like swags or bows. With this type of design, you need to calculate how many complete repeats will fit into each section of border space, then determine how large a space to leave between the repeats. The spacing may not be exactly the same for each wall, but as long as the differences are small, they will not be noticed. Sketch a master plan to guide you as you paint. Suppose the room measures 12 feet by 14 feet. If you want to do a swag border with 2-foot-long swags, you can fit exactly 6 swags on the 12-foot side and 7 swags on the 14-foot side. However, if the room measures 12 by 15 feet, then you are stuck with 7½ swags on the long side of the room, which will really spoil the effect. A better solution is to use the 24-inch swag on the short walls and cut a second stencil with the swag stretched out to 25.7 inches for the long wall. This will again give you 6 complete swags on one side and 7 on the other. If the stencil design is a loosely connected undulating vine or rosette with large gaps between the elements, instead of a continuous swag, you may not have to cut a different stencil for the problem wall. You may be able to get away with simply adding a 1½-inch gap between each stencil repeat. Try a paper proof and see how it looks before tackling the wall.

If you plan to put a border around a window frame or anything else that involves a sharp angle, you have to decide how to get the pattern around the corner. If you have ever done any quilting, some of the turning techniques will sound familiar. Doing a square-cut corner is just like doing a log-cabin quilt. Stencil the first section, stopping at the inner edge of the turn. Use masking tape or a piece of straight-cut paper to get a clean edge. Stencil the second section at right angles to the first, starting at the outside edge. Alternatively, you can both stop the first section and begin the second at the inside edge, filling the empty space with a corner motif. Then there is the mitred corner; cut a triangular piece of stencil material and use it as a mask, taping it on the surface before you stencil to create a clean 45-degree edge. Finally, you can fiddle with the pattern and design a corner piece that makes it look as though the border is wrapping around the corner.

The main difference between borders on walls and borders on napkins, tablecloths or Christmas cards is that you will eventually need to repaint the wall, and you may want to avoid redoing all the stencilled borders. The best way to accomplish this is to use some sort of

physical or visual device that completely separates the border design from the rest of the wall. For example, a frieze around the top of the walls might be physically divided from the lower part of the walls by a picture rail, a strip of moulding fastened high on the wall from which paintings can be hung. A visual separation would be a border edged with a painted stripe or with some form of uninterrupted stencilled edging. See Chapters Three and Four for examples of other stencils that can be used to enclose borders.

Most of these devices work best if the background of the stencilled border is a different colour or shade from the rest of the wall. Then, when you repaint the plain part of the wall, you need not worry about the new paint matching the old paint; all you need to do is repaint up to the edge of the stencilled border. If you want to repaint a room whose border is not separated from the rest of the wall, simply add a thin, striped horizontal edging to the border, then paint the wall a new colour up to the edging.

There are several ways to make striped edgings; all require measured guidelines. If you have a steady hand, you can make narrow stripes freehand with a thin lining or striping brush, following a pencil line measured out beforehand. There may be a small wobble to the line, but for some designs, a small wobble would not be out of place. To make a wider stripe, take a metal-edged ruler and a sharp knife and score the surface with two parallel lines that mark the width of your stripe. The scored tracks will help confine the paint

as you draw the brush along.

If the idea of striping freehand makes you nervous, you can always use stencils or masking tape. Take two strips of stiff stencil material cut from the outside edge of a factory-cut piece to give you truly straight edges, tape the strips down so that the straight edges coincide with the two guidelines of the stripe, and stencil in the paint evenly between them. A straight scrap of stencil material will help you get a clean edge at the end of the stripe. When you finish one section of the stripe, lift up the stencil strips, reposition them and do another section.

With masking tape, you can do fairly long stripes in one pass.

I find that the paint will often creep under masking tape just enough to create tiny flaws in a straight edge, but there is a way around this problem. Suppose you want a blue stripe on a cream background. First, tape both edges of the stripe. Then, paint a coat of the cream colour where you want the stripe to be and let it dry; this seals the edges of the masking tape to the wall. Finally, paint the blue between the strips of masking tape and gently remove the tape as soon as the blue has been laid down. If the stencilled border has a different background than the rest of the wall, seal the masking tape on each side of the stripe with the appropriate colour.

PLANNING A PROJECT

Once you have settled on a particular stencilling project (a baby quilt, thank-you notes or wall borders in the guest room), there are several things you need to plan before you can pick up a brush; most of these involve choosing or creating a design and planning its placement. Now that you have learned to cut your own stencils, you are no longer limited to whatever precut designs are available: you can copy from magazines or books, adapt patterns from textiles or teacups or use your imagination to create your own. However, before you get carried away with visions of heavenly cherubs floating across a cloud-dotted ceiling, trailing garlands of cabbage roses, there are a few guidelines to keep in mind.

First, the stencil you are planning should not be more ambitious than your abilities. If this is your first project and you want to save yourself a lot of grief, pick something that is easy to cut out and does not require either close registration or a dozen separate stencils. Here I speak from personal experience: although I kept my first project quite simple, in my second one, I threw all caution to the wind and ended up with over 20 stencils and a lot of tearing of hair and gnashing of teeth. The scope as well as the design of your first few projects should be modest, because you cannot avoid mistakes while you are learning. Ruining one Christmas card or one tea towel is much less stressful than having to repaint the living room 15 times to cover up your errors.

You also need to pick an appropriate size for your stencils—you might have to reduce the

pattern if it is for stationery or enlarge it if it is for a cushion or the yoke of an apron. Choosing the colours is also important. If you want to match a particular fabric or piece of furniture, you will probably have to mix your paints to get just the right hue.

Stencilling walls and floors generally calls for much more planning than other projects. Here, it is especially important to make sure the size or scale of the design fits the room. This is particularly true of borders. Narrow and delicate borders may look wonderful up close, but if they are not seen from that perspective, they will be lost. This is especially evident in photographs—borders that are not big enough seem to disappear when the wall is captured on film. Most examples of 19th-century stencilling, whether early American, Victorian or art nouveau, indicate borders of generous width—12 inches or more for friezes, for example.

Don't worry if your chosen design is three inches wide and you want a foot-wide frieze. The size of a pattern is easily manipulated with an enlarging photocopier. Or you can use the grid method to transfer and enlarge the design. I find this a lot faster to do if I mark the grids by carefully folding the paper instead of measuring and drawing endless sets of parallel and perpendicular lines.

Finally, consider the physical demands of the proposed project. Stencilling ceilings and high borders is very hard on the neck and shoulders. It also requires climbing up and down a ladder for almost every repeat of the design. Working close to the floor is equally demanding, espe-

cially for your back and knees. Wall borders anywhere from belly-button to eyeball level are relatively stress-free. Floors are always exhausting.

With large projects, unless you are planning something very simple like a regular, continuous border with no elements that need to be specially positioned—centred over the mantel, for example, or in the middle of the floor—you should make a scale drawing or a master plan on graph paper. A plan will allow you to play with the arrangement of motifs, prearrange any fudging of the spacing between design elements and even change the size of the motifs to make a better fit.

FOR COMPLEX PROJECTS SUCH AS THE BAY WINDOW BORDER, ABOVE, A MASTER PLAN HAD TO BE DRAWN TO SCALE ON GRAPH PAPER. THE LARGE FLORAL MOTIF, FACING PAGE, FIT PERFECTLY IN EACH CORNER, BUT IT REQUIRED CAREFUL PLANNING TO ARRANGE THE LEAF TENDRILS AND FLOWERS EVENLY IN BETWEEN. NOTE THAT THE FULL-BLOWN ROSE, THE BUD AND THE RIBBON ARE ELEMENTS TAKEN FROM THE STENCIL FOR THE CORNER MOTIF.

completely confident in my choice of border but found it too busy when it looked down on me from all four walls. I painted out most of it, then started putting up one-metre sections of different designs for comparison. At one point, there were more than a dozen different sections of frieze surrounding the room, and I was in utter despair, immobilized by indecision. Finally, I simply painted everything out, and the room is still quite plain, awaiting a flash of inspiration. The moral of the story is: don't worry if you change your mind about something you have just stencilled, but do be sure to reserve enough wall paint so that you can paint the design out without redoing the entire wall.

By this time, you will be more than impatient with all these preliminaries. You want to see the finished item right there in front of you. Now comes the most discouraging part of the whole project: you are all set to start, but you realize that you really should repaint the wall, sand the floor or strip the furniture first. On my first project, I ended up not only painting the wall but patching, sanding and priming cracks, sanding woodwork and installing tongue-and-groove wainscotting as well. The preparation took weeks, the stencilling hours. You don't have to do a lot of preparation, but if you don't, you will probably wish you had.

One learns a craft by making mistakes, and the way I learned to stencil was no exception. As with most enthusiastic beginners, my first efforts were overly ambitious, but in terms of learning, they were profitable. Here

Once you have picked a design, planned its placement, scaled it to the right size, decided how to turn any corners and cut the stencils, you should make some paper proofs. I like to use rolled shelf paper for this—it is cheap and yields a nice unbroken length for trying out borders. Whatever you use, print a few yards of the border or the overall design. Then tape it to the wall, the floor or the side of the blanket box, and let it stay there for several days. You will have a chance to evaluate the design, the colour and its placement. If you start to feel uneasy about any of these, make the changes, and again let the proofs stay there until you have decided it is right. I once left a paper proof pinned to the kitchen

wall for a year, unable to make up my mind. If you think it likely that you will be making changes to the first draft of your design, make the draft stencil out of something cheaper and easier to cut than Mylar—stiff paper, for example.

Sometimes a paper proof seems fine, but after stencilling the whole thing right on the wall, you find you don't like it anymore. It may be because of the different background or the effect of continuous repeats all around the room or it may be nothing more than simply changing your mind. This dilemma is one I face more often than I care to admit, possibly because I often skip the proof stage. When I repainted our living room last year, I started off

are some of the things I learned:
• If you use a chalk line to mark a guideline on a wall, keep a minimum amount of chalk in the container, and try to get a colour similar to the wall's. Make your own chalk, if necessary, by grating coloured blackboard chalks or using powdered poster paints. Once, when I first started stencilling, I loaded my chalk line with a whole package of bright blue chalk and snapped it against a white wall; I never did get it all off.
• Don't leave masking tape on the wall for a week and expect it to come off without taking a piece of the wall finish with it.
• Japan paint dissolves foam plates and turns black in metal ones. I will not describe the mess I made learning that.
• If you tell yourself that you do not need to tape each stencil in place, either you will slip, the phone will ring or your brush will go dry in the middle of executing the stencil.
• The job will always take at least twice as long as you think it will. This means that you could be partway through when you have to leave to pick up the kids at school. To keep paint and brushes from drying out, cover the paint saucer tightly with plastic wrap, and put each brush in a plastic sandwich bag along with a folded-up piece of paper towel dampened (not wet) with solvent. If you are still worried, put it all in the fridge to keep cool, but make sure everything is well sealed, or the eggs and butter will be contaminated by the smell of turpentine.
• You can mix colours to get exactly what you want. To japan paint, I add small amounts of artist's oil colours, available at hobby and art-supply stores, and to water- or oil-based paints, I add universal tints, available from paint stores. The batches that do not end up quite right, I save in old baby-food jars. If you mix your own colours, make sure that you prepare more than enough for the whole project, because you will never get exactly the same shade again. Even if you buy ready-mixed colours, you must be wary there can be noticeable differences from one lot to another.
• Finally, always put the lid back on the paint jar after taking out the small amount needed for the palette. An open jar will not only dry out the paint; it is an invitation for a messy spill.

CHAPTER TWO

STEP-BY-STEP EXERCISES

This chapter will teach you all the basic techniques required to become an accomplished stenciller. It begins with the simplest of exercises, using one stencil and one colour, then gradually progresses, adding one new step or technique with each exercise. If you are a complete beginner, you should start with the first exercise and work your way through them all. (It's a lot of fun, so don't look on it as a chore!) If you have already tried your hand at stencilling, you may want to do only the exercises on techniques that are unfamiliar to you.

Full-size reproductions of the designs discussed in the text are found in the illustrations that accompany each exercise. The easiest way to use the designs is to photocopy them, tape them to the Mylar and cut them out directly as described on pages 20-21. If you do not intend to reuse the stencils, make them out of something cheaper and less durable than Mylar—stiff paper, for example, or clear Mactac.

Practise all these exercises on paper—computer paper, scrap paper or shelf paper—until you achieve consistent results. (I use fabric paint for this.) Only then should you actually undertake a project. Although these exercises will teach you all you really need to know, the only way to become proficient is through practice, and practising on paper is the easiest and cheapest way of honing your skills. Don't be discouraged when you make mistakes. It is the best way to learn.

EXERCISE ONE: ONE STENCIL, ONE COLOUR

FLEUR-DE-LIS

"One stencil, one colour" may sound boring, but you'll be surprised at what you can do with such basic materials. Even if this is all you ever learn to do, it is enough to make elegant borders, quilts and greeting cards. Let us begin with one of the most ancient decorative motifs, the fleur-de-lis. One of the most common heraldic symbols, it was the emblem of the French royal family (which is undoubtedly why it does not appear on the flag of the Republic of France) and the symbol of French sovereignty in New France. Even after New France was ceded to the English, the fleur-de-lis found its way onto the coat of arms and the flag of the province of Quebec.

Before you decide how big a piece of stencil material to use for the fleur-de-lis, read through the rest of the exercise, since you may want to buy a piece large enough to accommodate several repeats of the pattern. First, cut a single fleur-de-lis out of the stencil, place it over a piece of practice paper and tape it down at the corners. Following the method described on page 24, get some paint on the end of the brush, work it around evenly on the bristles, wipe off any excess, take a deep breath and apply paint to paper through the holes in the stencil. If you have any problems, go back and reread the section on applying paint. Practise the fleur-de-lis a few times until you get the hang of it. For anyone interested in bronze-powder stencilling, this is a good design to practise with. Clean the stencil, read the instructions on page 50 and bronze the fleur-de-lis on dark paper.

POWDERED DESIGN

In the next part of the exercise, use the same stencil to paint a "powdered" design, an overall pattern created with multiple repetitions of a simple motif that is laid out formally but without direct connections between the prints.

To make powdering easy, you need a simple, convenient way of positioning each print. You can draw a grid on the paper — or on the wall, should you decide to use this exercise as a wall decoration — but it is easier to put a few repeat registration marks on the stencil and only enough guidelines on the paper (or wall) that you do not slowly work your way out of alignment as you stencil across the surface (on a wall, a 1/16-inch error adds up if there are 150 prints). To paint the powdered design, position the stencil and make the first print. Lift the stencil and reposition it so that the print aligns with one of the repeat registration outlines. Make a second print. Continue, working systematically across, up and down the surface to be covered. If you plan on covering a large area, it would be worth the effort to cut more than one motif on a single sheet of Mylar, because it will save time moving and repositioning the stencil. Stencils with long curves or unstable parts are easier to control when sprayed on the back with a little temporary adhesive such as 3M Spray Mount.

COUNTRY CHECK

Now that you have done an overall pattern, a one-colour, one-stencil border will seem easy. Here is a simple one to start with—a country check that is easy to cut out and to execute. It can be used on its own, in a variety of sizes or as a border edging above and below another motif. You can cut this stencil freehand, without using a straight edge, because none of the edges are perfectly straight. Since the corners are slightly rounded, adjacent squares do not touch.

To print the border, position the stencil for the first print, lin-ing up the horizontal guideline on the stencil with the chalk line on the wall or the marking you have made on the paper to guide the positioning of the border. Paint the first print. As always, start by applying the paint sparingly. Lift a corner of the stencil to check the darkness of the print. If it is too light, apply a little more paint. When it is satisfactory, lift off the stencil. The paint dries almost immediately, so don't worry about smudging it. Reposition the stencil, lining up the horizontal guideline and positioning the repeat registration marks over the last part of the first print.

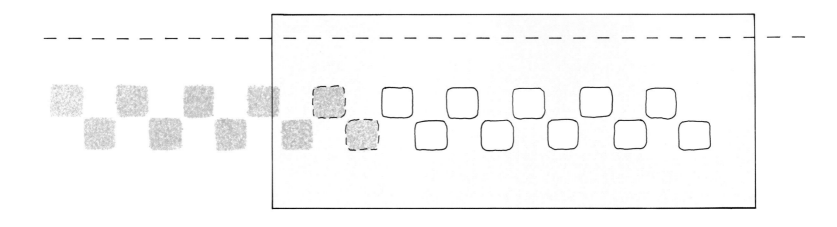

SILHOUETTE PRINTS

Simple one-colour stencils can be used in interesting, beautiful ways. For example, instead of cutting a flower out of the Mylar, leave the flower intact and cut out the background. The resulting silhouette prints—the negative images of a design—can be most attractive; they have a very solid feeling about them, especially when done as a border, because of the relatively continuous flow of monochromatic colour. The only trick in designing them is to manipulate the shape of the silhouette so that it just touches the edge of the background in enough places to give the whole thing some structural stability. You will understand what I mean after you have done a few that don't hold together properly. When you try this stencil, experiment a bit with the background; for instance, try shading it unevenly or blending from one hue to a related one and back again. You can also lay down a band of colour before you stencil so that the silhouette is a different colour than either the negative-image background or the surface that you stencil on.

EXERCISE TWO: TWO STENCILS, ONE COLOUR

Sometimes you need to use two or more stencils for a single design, even if only one colour is used. This is the case with designs that have bridges so narrow that the Mylar is unlikely to survive multiple prints—for example, a chessboard or checkered border with squares and rectangles of colour that almost touch. You will also need two stencils for designs with overlapping parts that eliminate bridges altogether—as in the petals of an opening rosebud. Using two stencils also allows you to give the impression of structure by overprinting certain parts, such

as the veins on a leaf or the grooves on a scallop shell.

CHECKERED BORDER

For the checkered border, make one stencil for the small squares and a second for the horizontal rectangles. Tape the first stencil in position. Apply paint, then remove the stencil. Position the second stencil, using registration marks to line it up with respect to the part already printed. Apply paint, then remove the stencil. Although the elements of the design are virtually touching, separate stencils ensure that all the corners are crisp and well defined.

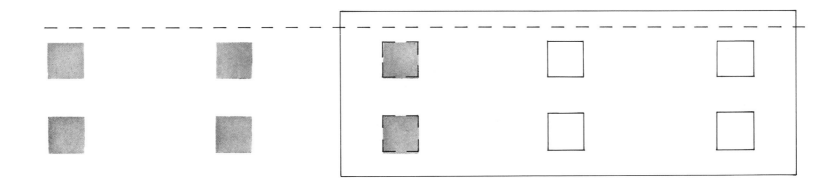

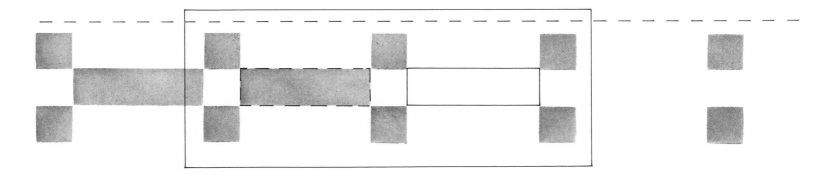

FLOWERS

Flowers with overlapping petals are done the same way, except that you must be careful not to make either print too dark; otherwise, you will not be able to see the overlap. The two stencils for this type of design are sometimes identical except for the registration marks. Print the first stencil lightly but with well-defined edges. Position the second stencil and apply paint, again using a light touch and making sure that the edges are crisp. It is very easy to make one of the prints too dark, which spoils the translucent effect of the overlapping petals. This technique works best with paint that is more transparent, such as japan or fabric paint.

SCALLOP SHELL

Finally, to make the scallop shell, print the first stencil fairly lightly but with the outside edge darker than the middle. Then position the second stencil. The print for it should be dark but, again, with the middle part of the shell lighter than the rest.

EXERCISE THREE: TWO STENCILS, TWO COLOURS

VICTORIAN BORDER

For most designs, you will need a separate stencil for each colour. This is to ensure that each colour ends up only on the parts for which it was planned and does not get brushed onto other parts of the design. The only tricky part is positioning the stencils so that the two colours end up in the right places. But with transparent stencils, even this part is easy. For this exercise, a stylized Victorian flowered border, there are two stencils, one for the green leaves and a second for the red berries, but the same method applies whether there are 2 or 12 colours in a design.

I usually prefer to print the stencil with the largest part of the design first—in this case, the one for the leaves. Tape it in place, apply the paint and lift the stencil. Usually it is best to finish all the repeats of the first colour before going on to the second. This avoids problems with paint drying on the brush, the palette and the stencil while you are switching colours. It also prevents you from accidentally putting the green brush into the red paint. But what is a rule without exceptions? I often find that I am so eager to see what the completed design looks like that I do both colours in parallel.

For the time being, however, print a few more repeats of the first stencil, lining it up carefully using the repeat registration marks. Now position the berry stencil over the first print of the leaves, using the colour registration marks to line up the two elements in the design. Apply paint, remove the stencil and repeat until finished. This border is very forgiving: you can be a fair bit out of alignment in the repeats and the positioning of the second colour, and the final result will still look fine.

ART DECO BORDER

Country designs and early-American patterns are generally imprecise in terms of alignment, so they are ideal for the inexperienced stenciller to begin with. Here is a more modern two-colour design that is an exception to the general rule of one stencil for each colour. The middle and the outside triangles of the chevron are printed in the same colour, but because they meet at a point and there are no bridges between them, two stencils are required. Printing each motif is therefore a three-step process.

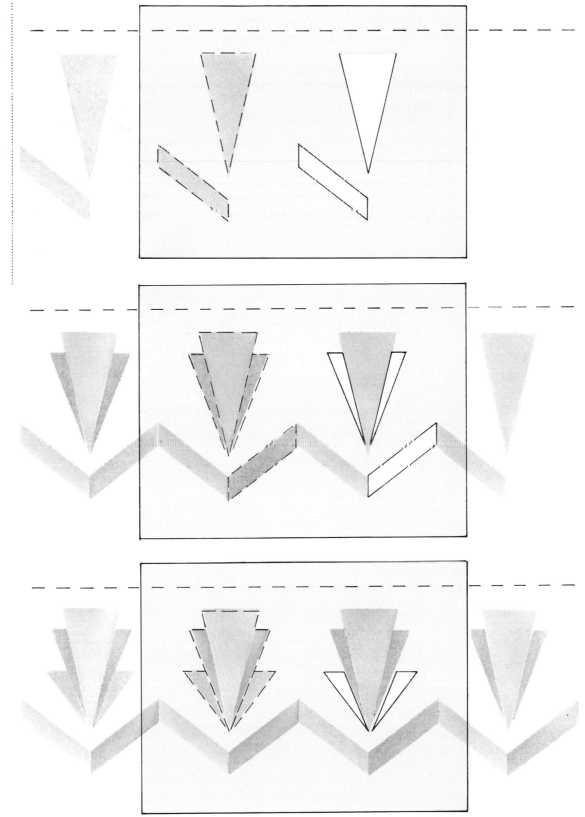

EXERCISE FOUR: ONE STENCIL, TWO COLOURS

Some two-colour motifs have enough of a bridge or separation between the differently coloured parts of the design that they can be executed with only one stencil. In fact, most commercial precut stencils—unless they are quite expensive—are manufactured as single units. If you want to paint a one-stencil design in more than one colour, cover the part of the stencil that will be pink while you paint the green and vice versa. If the bridges are wide, this is no problem: you simply stick masking tape over the appropriate part of the design. But sometimes the bridges are so small and finicky that it drives you crazy trying to stick bits of tape over the parts you do not want to paint. Thus, only certain designs—those with large, well-dispersed elements—are appropriate for the one-stencil, two-colour technique.

By now, you should be getting the idea of what is involved in these exercises, so I will simplify the instructions. Cut the floral stencil as illustrated and tape it in position. You only have to do this once. If the gap between the colours seems narrow or if you are using a large brush, protect the part of the stencil you are not painting with a piece of masking tape, cardboard or Mylar. Then paint the leaves one colour and the rosebuds another. When finished, reposition the stencil and repeat, painting both colours as you go.

Some stencillers deliberately use just one stencil for multicoloured images because they like the way colours blend wherever there is a bridge between cutouts of different hues. Try painting this stencil again, this time shading some leaf colour onto the flower and vice versa.

EXERCISE FIVE: SHADING

Shading lends a more three-dimensional effect to an image, which is useful if you are using stencils for trompe-l'oeils or murals. For period decoration, make sure the shading is appropriate, for in most cases, stencilled images were painted quite flat, with little definition. When painting the five examples illustrated, it is important that the brush be quite dry. These examples are also good exercises for stencil work done with metallic powders, since it is almost always shaded.

SPHERE

To shade a round object, start by working the brush around the edge, trying to get an even colour. Gradually work inward with an ever-lighter touch so that the colour fades to almost nothing in the centre. Use the same technique for anything round—balloons, apples, teddy-bear tummies, fat geese.

CYLINDER

For objects that are more cylindrical than round, start painting along the long edges and lighten up as you work inward. You should end up with a long, thin light area, parallel to the sides but not necessarily exactly in the middle.

LEAF

This two-part stencil lets you show something of the structure of a leaf without actually painting any veins. Paint the first half of the leaf, making the lower edge darker than the top (the top is really the centre of the leaf). Now paint the second part of the leaf, again making the lower edge darker than the top (this time, the lower edge is the centre of the leaf).

FLOWER

Shaded flowers are characteristic of early New England counterpanes or bedspreads. First, apply paint or powder evenly around the outer edges, then work gradually inward with an ever-lighter touch. A small brush will give you better control over the shading. The most common mistake is getting the centres too dark; they can be almost bare of colour. Complete the centres of the flowers by overpainting a few stamens or by using single-edged stencils to create petal outlines as described in Exercises Six and Seven.

LEAF BORDER

Borders made up of overlapping leaves were used a great deal on early-American stencilled chairs and on Victorian papier-mâché trays. They are very easy to do and look especially attractive in bronze on a dark background. For a border, stencil a single leaf, shading in only the tip and sides of the leaf and leaving the stem part unpainted. Move the stencil slightly to the left (it should overlap the unpainted part of the first image) and repeat. If you want an exact overlap, you can use repeat registration marks, but I usually simply eyeball the design.

EXERCISE SIX: OVERPAINTING

Stencilling details or highlights on top of previously stencilled areas usually works very well if the top colour is either brighter or darker than the one underneath and if the two colours together do not produce some ghastly hue. For tiny details such as flower stamens and leaf veins, I like to use thin stencil material that is easy to cut, like paper or Mactac. These stencils do not need to be robust, and they are very finicky to cut out otherwise.

STRAWBERRY 1

Stencil the stem and sepals of the berry in green and the general form of the berry in red. The outer edges of the berry should be crisp and dark and the inside shaded lighter to suggest roundness. Now, stencil the berry details in dark, unshaded red on top of the first red.

STRAWBERRY 2

This berry has some of the green sepals overlapping the fruit. Unless you use a very opaque paint, putting red on top of green, or vice versa, will produce brown. The solution here is to shade the top of each berry so that it fades into nothing. The green, applied second, remains true because it overlaps very little red.

APPLE

If you are using colours that are even slightly transparent, you can sometimes use overpainting to get an extra colour without making an extra stencil. For ex-

ample, paint this apple and its stem red. Then paint the leaf and stem green. The stem gets painted twice—red and green—and *voilà*, it comes out brown.

PEACH

Sometimes you can use overpainting to suggest shape. You have already seen a one-colour example of this with the scallop shell in Exercise Two. The peach example uses two colours, one for the undertone and a different one for the shading. Start by painting the first stencil of the peach a golden yellow, shading it darker around the outside and quite light at the centre. Now, stipple a blush of pink or red around part of the outside. Lift the first stencil, position the second one, and stipple the same blush along its edge to define the crease of the peach.

VEINED LEAF

Start with a leaf that is well defined around the outside and lightly shaded toward the centre so that the veins will show. There are several ways to add veins: use a fine, tapered paintbrush, and paint the veins freehand; cut a vein stencil; or use a single-edged stencil as described in Exercise Seven. Instead of overpainting veins, you can also cut them out of Mactac and carefully stick them in the middle of the leaf stencil before making a print. The veins will show as a negative image the same colour as the background.

48

EXERCISE SEVEN: SINGLE-EDGED STENCILS

Single-edged stencils are simply shaped edges of stencil material. You can use them to create silhouettes, borders or details within another stencil; for example, clouds in a mural, a scalloped border or leaf veins in a chair-back design. The technique is the same for all of them. Position the stencil, then apply paint evenly along the edge, shading away to nothing a slight distance away from the stencil (for a narrow border, you need a small brush). It is essential to have the brush quite dry so that you can taper the shading quickly. With bronzing, you need only run your velvet-covered finger gently along the edge of the stencil.

LANDFORMS
An irregular curved edge can be used to create background landforms such as hills or mountains. Use them for murals or chair-back landscapes.

WAVES
Use a scalloped edge to build up a stretch of wavy water, either as part of a mural or underneath a border of boats. The spacing should be irregular, but in general, the wave crests in the distance should be closer together. Paint the peaks or the troughs of the waves using either a convex or a concave edge.

FLOWERS
A folk-art rose can be built up with a single scalloped edge applied several times to the interior of a flower outline.

VEINED LEAF
Use a curved edge and a narrow brush to paint dark green veins on pale stencilled leaves. Trim one edge of the leaf stencil to the shape required so that whenever you stencil the leaf, the veining edge will be handy.

EXERCISE EIGHT: BRONZING A COMPOSITE DESIGN

Early-19th-century Canadian and American chair backs were often decorated by means of composite stencils—separate stencils for each fruit or flower of an overall design. The elements were arranged and stencilled individually (often with very delicate shading) so that the design was built up gradually. For example, to paint a bunch of grapes, there might be two stencils that were simply circles of different sizes; the bunch would be built up by stencilling one circle at a time, positioning each in an ad hoc manner. Composite designs were sometimes stencilled in colour, but more often, they were done with bronze powders. On later, factory-produced chairs, composite stencilling gave way to cruder designs done with all-in-one stencils and a minimum of shading in order to speed up production.

One of the few hobbies considered socially acceptable for well-bred young ladies of the 19th century was called theorem painting, and it also entailed the use of composite stencils (the stencils were called theorems). Theorem painting was nothing more than painting on velvet, but instead of the 20th-century versions of fiery tropical sunsets and teary-eyed urchins on black velvet, the subject matter was usually limited to bowls of fruit and baskets of flowers.

To create a composite design using bronze powder, start with the centre foreground and work outward, tapering the shading of adjacent elements so that they seem to pass behind the foreground. To begin, cut stencils for leaves, tendrils, a stem and circles of various sizes to represent the grapes. Apply a thin coat of varnish to a black background. When the varnish is dry enough, stencil the grape stem and large leaves as shown. Next, stencil the central grapes as complete circles. Now build up the bunch of grapes one by one, working from the centre to the edge of the bunch. Taper each grape to nothing at the point where it disappears behind its neighbour. You do not need to copy my composition—just build up the grapes so that the final bunch looks fairly natural. Start with a general idea of how you want the grapes to look, and just keep filling them in until the whole thing seems balanced. Finally, fill in the pattern with leaves or tendrils if you wish.

Landscape designs are built up in the same way, except that the order of adding elements may take more planning. The best approach is to practise a few times on paper, and when you have a satisfactory composition, mark numbers on the different elements to indicate the order in which they should be added.

A touch of luminous, glowing colour can be added to bronzed stencilling by loosely brushing a wash or glaze over parts of the finished design. Cut out the stencils. Apply a uniform coat of varnish to black paper or black-painted practice board. When the varnish is almost dry, position the stencils and apply silver-coloured powder. After stencilling, let everything dry for 24 hours. For the colour wash, mix some varnish with a tiny amount of artist's oil colour or japan paint, and using an artist's brush of an appropriate size, spread a light wash of colour over the bronzing. Paint the entire composition one colour, or paint each flower a different hue; for example, create an antique blue by mixing Prussian blue with a touch of raw umber and a dusty rose by mixing crimson and raw umber. Paint the leaves with a green-and-raw-umber-tinted varnish.

CHAPTER THREE

PROJECTS

Even if you never get beyond the stage of practising on paper, you can still derive a good deal of fun and mileage from stencilling. All sorts of paper articles—stationery, greeting cards, wrapping paper, trinket boxes, bookmarks—can be decorated without too much effort, expense or mess. I usually stencil wrapping paper, Christmas cards and birthday-party invitations (this is always a joint project, in which my sons help with the design and production). Paper projects are excellent to begin with because they are small, the materials are relatively cheap and disposable and the end results are as useful as they are unique—one can never have too much wrapping paper or too many cards. The projects described in this chapter become increasingly complex and run the stencilling gamut from simple paper greeting cards to floor mats, tablecloths, fake tiles and children's furniture. In each case, the sample stencil motifs are accompanied by a photograph of a finished project incorporating the designs. Many are interchangeable, with pillow patterns showing up on hat boxes and quilt designs doubling as gift tags.

PAPER PROJECTS

Although stencilled paper items are appropriate at any time of year, there is something about the months preceding the Christmas season that unleashes the creative urge. Whether it is nostalgia for an old-fashioned, homemade kind of Christmas or a need to economize or simply a desire to tone down the commercial aspects of the holiday, pre-Christmas months are like no others for inspiring us to make things with our hands. Stencils are a wonderful tool for creating greeting cards, gift tags, tree decorations and wrapping paper or for embellishing tablecloths (paper or cloth), tree skirts and Christmas stockings. It is so easy that youngsters can help too. Children love to use stencils. Let them decorate their own gift wrappings and tree decorations. Young children can use sponges to apply the paint, or for even less mess, they can stencil with crayons, felt pens or bingo markers (felt pens with a large round pad instead of a tip).

The designs for paper projects included here can be used as is or modified—you can put several motifs together to make something more complex or simplify the design by removing some elements. Change the size to suit your needs by using a photocopier that enlarges and reduces. Do not be afraid to adapt designs for borders to personalize stationery or bookmarks. The bamboo pattern on the left, facing page, is based on an old Japanese stencil design, whereas the borders, centre and right, were borrowed from 16th-century book bindings.

Always bear in mind, though, that while you may feel inspired to create a Christmas card or

wedding invitation that requires 10 stencils to print, you may not feel quite so enthusiastic when you are halfway through printing the 200 cards that you need. Try not to use too many colours: limit yourself to one or two with, at most, a small accent of a third colour. Some of the colour choices will be obvious, but don't hesitate to experiment with unusual combinations.

There is only one important thing to remember when you stencil on paper: it is not nearly as tough as a floor or a wall. To avoid disturbing the surface of the paper, stencil brushes should be quite soft and flexible, and you should start with a light touch as you move the brush over the paper. Be careful not to overwork any one area. Even though the paint seems uneven with the stencil still in place, the design will look fine once the stencil is lifted; in fact, it will probably look better with the paint uneven. Since some paper is easily damaged, do not use masking tape to hold down the stencil. Often you can work quickly by simply holding the stencil against the paper with one hand. If you have trouble holding the stencil still, try using Scotch Magic Plus removable tape. You can also spray a little temporary adhesive on the back of the stencil.

If the paper is particularly delicate—as it usually is in napkins and tissue paper—you may have to stipple or sponge on the paint. Experiment with different methods of application until you find one that works and gives an interesting texture.

If you are using stencil paint, almost any kind of paper will do, since the paint dries instantaneously and will not bleed. If you use felt pens, you will need a paper that doesn't bleed. I prefer to use fabric paints (I use Stencil Ease or Adele Bishop) for paper stencilling: they go on very smoothly and can be used for both translucent and opaque effects. However, to get a really crisp white on a bright background, I resort to acrylic paint, which is more opaque.

GREETING CARDS

For greeting cards, choose paper with a thickness or weight that feels similar to that of a typical card. Hobby and stationery stores usually carry either blank cards or sheets of heavy bond writing paper that you can fold to make into cards. Alternatively, you can buy a pad of drawing or art paper to cut and fold into cards. Plan the final dimensions of the card carefully, because you will need envelopes for the cards and envelopes come in only a few standard sizes. If you buy paper and envelopes separately, it is a good idea to buy the envelopes first, then pick a card size to fit.

If you are cutting your own cards from sheets or pads of paper, you may find it difficult to cut a perfectly straight line with scissors. A paper cutter is more satisfactory, but do not try to cut many sheets at the same time: they tend to slide out of alignment. I prefer to use a rotary cutting wheel, sold in fabric shops as a quilter's tool for cutting strips of cloth. Working on a cutting board, I position a metal-edged ruler along the line I wish to cut, hold it down firmly and slide the cutter along the edge. This way, I can cut several sheets of paper at the same time.

Once you have decided on the size and shape of the greeting card, trace the outer dimensions onto tracing paper. From the designs in this chapter (or any that you wish to create yourself), select one or more motifs and move it (or them) around under the tracing paper until you have a pleasing arrangement within the rectangular outline of the card. Now trace the overall design onto the tracing paper.

With coloured pencils or felt pens, shade in the colours you want to use. When you have decided how many stencils you need and which part of the design belongs to each stencil, you are ready to cut. Make sure that the Mylar extends at least ¼ inch beyond the edges of the card. For colour registration, mark the outside edges of the card on the Mylar with a fine-tipped permanent felt pen or with a scratch from the stencil-cutting knife.

If you want to print a fairly large number of greeting cards, you can save time by constructing a right-angled corner guide from pieces of heavy cardboard or from layers of masking tape; it should be the same thickness as the card. Attach the corner guide securely to the work surface. To stencil, push a card firmly into the V of the guide. Position the first stencil over the card, and tape the stencil to the table or to the guide so that it is hinged on one side. Print the card, raise the stencil, remove the printed card, push a new card into the corner, lower the stencil and print. Continue in this way until all cards have been printed with the first stencil, then repeat the process for the other stencils, building up the design until all the cards are finished.

GIFT TAGS

Depending on the shape and size of the cards and the piece of paper they are cut from, you may find yourself with dozens of leftover strips of heavy paper. Don't throw them out; they make excellent gift tags or name cards for the dinner table. You can even use some of the design motifs here to turn the paper scraps into bookmarks for the avid readers on your gift list.

WRAPPING PAPER

Instead of buying expensive wrapping paper and ribbon, you can custom-stencil your own from plain white shelf paper, leftover computer paper, brown kraft paper or even cut-up paper grocery bags turned inside out to conceal the store's logo. If the gift to be wrapped is soft, you will have to stencil the paper first. If the gift is fairly rigid or is contained in a box, then wrap it first with the plain paper, using a minimum of tape. Now you can position the stencilled images to their best advantage. For example, paint a motif in each corner and then work an overall pattern in toward the centre. Don't bother to measure the placement of each image. For gift wrapping, you can do quite well just by eyeballing.

Perfectly plain gift boxes can be stencilled directly, which eliminates the need to use any wrapping paper at all. Try using inexpensive off-white bakery boxes. If you can unfold the boxes, do so, since it is easier to stencil them flat. Another very inexpensive idea is to use brown paper lunch bags (you can buy packages of them in supermarkets) as gift bags. Stencil a border all around the bag or paint a large motif on each side. Make holes near the top with a paper punch, thread ribbon through the holes and tie it in a bow.

GIFT BOWS

Gift ribbon can be quite expensive, and if you send a package by mail, the bow is inevitably flattened. A stencilled bow, however, is flat from the start, no matter how fancy it is. Decorate gifts using ribbon and bow stencils; add a nosegay of flowers or a sprig of holly to embellish it for Christmas.

TABLECLOTHS

Plain white paper tablecloths (about $2 each) can be stencilled, but they must be painted very carefully, as the paper is not very strong. Try one of the larger motifs in this chapter or Chapter Six as the main part of the border, and enclose it within a narrow border of poinsettia or holly for Christmas or of flowers or checks for a summer birthday picnic. You can stencil a small border near the bottom edge, then place the cloth on the table and stencil a second border just inside the edge of the tabletop. Consider stencilling matching napkins at the same time, using a small motif from the tablecloth design and applying it in one corner or as a border around the edge of the napkin. The tablecloth illustrated was stencilled with a motif derived from the pattern on the pottery dishes, creating a truly custom-decorated table.

FABRIC PROJECTS

QUILTS AND PILLOWS

In 19th-century New England, counterpanes were often decorated with stencilled motifs, which offered an instantaneous way of achieving the effect of elaborate appliqués. Well, maybe not exactly instantaneous, but compared with the effort involved in cutting, piecing and handstitching all those pieces of material, stencilling is very fast indeed. To make stencilled quilts look almost like the real thing, use traditional appliqué patterns and colours to stencil the top fabric, then assemble the quilt with batting between the printed top and the backing and quilt around the stencilled images. The quilted fabric can be fashioned into blankets, bedspreads or pillows.

Of course, you don't have to stick to traditional designs. For baby quilts, you might prefer piglets or Peter Rabbits or teddy bears (see Chapter Four). Whatever the design, I find that stencilled quilts look best with very simple piecing, square stencilled blocks alternating in checkerboard fashion with pieces of calico fabric. For something that involves less sewing but more stencilling, you might consider making an unpieced, unquilted bedspread, after the fashion of early-American counterpanes.

If you want to try a really small-scale fabric project but something a little more appealing than a toaster cover, why not try a miniature quilt? Miniature quilts are made just like big ones, except that everything is much smaller. These small-scale reproductions have enormous appeal because they are not only visually attractive but

also much less tedious, cumbersome and expensive to create. What, you might ask, does one do with a quilt only 15 inches long? They are obviously not very useful for keeping you warm at night. They do, however, make delightful doll quilts, place mats or wall decorations, and they are a quick and inexpensive way of trying out designs and colour combinations for a full-sized quilt.

QUILTING INSTRUCTIONS

The following instructions are for quilts of any size, whether the blocks are 12 inches across or 2. Before you begin, take a pencil and a piece of paper, make a scale drawing of the quilt and decide on the size of the finished quilt, the size of each block and the number of blocks you need. You should then be able to calculate how much fabric you need—plain cotton for the stencilled squares, calico for the other squares and for the backing (or you can use plain backing if you wish). Don't forget to include the seam allowances around the blocks when figuring out the total amount of fabric needed. Quarter-inch seams are standard, but I always use the edge of my presser foot as a guide; it produces a wider, ⅜-inch seam but saves me having to measure. Wash the fabric to preshrink it and to remove any sizing. Adjust the size of the design to fit the block size, and cut the appropriate stencils.

I find it easier to stencil all the blocks on one piece of cotton first and then cut them into individual blocks. It eliminates the problem of making an uncorrectable stencilling mistake after you have done all the work of piecing. There are two ways to mark out the blocks:

1. Use a ruler and a fabric marker or ballpoint pen to rule the quilt blocks (including seam allowances) on the cloth, taking care to line them up with the grain of the fabric.

2. With a steam iron, press creases to delineate the squares (again including seam allowances). I prefer this method to using a marker, because if I make a mistake or change my

mind, it is easy to iron out all the folds and start over again.

The stencilled image should be nicely balanced in the middle of the block, so mark a guideline on the stencil that matches the outside edges of the block (not the seamline). Tape or staple the prepared fabric to a work board, making sure the grain of the cloth is straight. Following the instructions for fabric stencilling on pages 26-27, stencil each block. Do a few extra, just in case something unforeseen happens. Cut the blocks along the marked lines, let them dry for a few days, then heat-set according to the instructions that come with the paint.

Piece the blocks together, alternating stencilled prints with calico. Press the seams toward the calico. If you follow quilting tradition, you will have an odd number of blocks in each row and an odd number of rows. Some rows start and end with stencilled blocks, some with calico ones. Make sure you have the right number of each by laying them out in position on a flat surface ahead of time.

Now stitch the rows together, matching seams carefully. The finished rows will be easy to piece together if you have been consistent in pressing the seams, because matching seam allowances should face in opposite directions. Press the quilt top, add whatever borders you want and press again. Make the usual quilt sandwich with backing, batting and quilt top, and baste them together thoroughly. Use tiny, even running stitches to quilt through all thicknesses. Quilt adjacent to seams or along the outline of stencilled areas. Finally, bind the edges.

SEAM ALLOWANCE

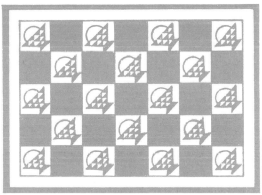

FLOOR CLOTHS

Historically, fabric was also used to cover the floor, and floor cloths, as they were called, were often stencilled. The evolution of floor cloths is discussed on pages 114-115, but although it is a very old form of stencilling, you need not feel confined to historically accurate designs. Think of it as an artistic expression that you can walk on. If you do not feel all that artistic, some of the most stunning floor cloths are stencilled versions of 19th-century quilts. I have included a traditional and a modern pattern here, and the library will have many more in books on quilting and pioneer handicrafts. Simple motifs in bright colours are ideal for stencilling. If you want to try out the technique before committing yourself to a large project, make a few place mats. Or create a floor mat that is a landscape map for the children to use with toy cars, trucks and train sets (see page 87). It can be rolled up and put away when not in use.

The finished floor cloth will be flat and quite stiff, so it is not really a substitute for a soft rug. As a covering for a firm surface, such as a bare floor or porch, a floor cloth is very durable and easy to clean, but if it is placed on top of carpeting and then walked on, it may suffer small surface cracks.

The best material for a floor cloth is untreated cotton canvas in a weight that feels substantial but is still pliable enough to fold for a hem. Canvas shrinks a little when it is primed (unless it can be stretched during priming), and you need to allow 1½ to 2 inches for hemming on all sides, so determine the amount you need to buy accordingly. Allow a little bit extra just in case you measure wrong. Many art-supply stores sell canvas by the yard in widths of up to four feet. Sometimes it is available already primed. If you look in the Yellow Pages under Canvas Goods, you may be able to find even wider canvas, at least up to six feet wide. To get the canvas home from the store, roll it up—do not fold it. Once home, trim off the selvages and remove any creases with a steam iron.

To make a floor cloth, you need a clean, flat work surface, one that is big enough to accommodate the canvas. A large tabletop might do for a mat, but for large projects, you will need a floor cleared of furniture and protected with a drop cloth and barricaded against dogs, cats and small children. The project will take several days to complete, so make sure the chosen work space can be reserved for that long. North American women in the 1830s and 1840s were instructed in homemaking books and magazines to stretch and nail their cloth to the south side of the barn, then to let each priming coat dry for two weeks and the final coat for at least two months. I do not have a barn, but sometimes I staple the canvas to the unfinished drywall in our basement.

Fortunately, modern paints do not need two months on the sunny side of a barn to dry, so this project will only take a few days instead of the better part of a season. Prime the canvas with several coats of latex paint in a background colour – the more coats of primer, the smoother and tougher the floor cloth will be. I give the underside a priming coat too.

Sketch out a master plan for the floor cloth, showing the placement and colours for each stencil, then make a paper proof of the whole thing, if it is small, or of each motif, if it is large. If you are unhappy with the overall arrangement, cut out individual paper motifs and move them around on the canvas until you come up with something you like. When you are happy with the design, go ahead and stencil onto the canvas, using masking

tape, Scotch removable tape or tiny pencil dots to mark whatever guidelines are needed. I like to start in the middle and work outward, leaving the border until last so that if I make any mistakes in measurement or alignment, I can adjust the size of the border to compensate.

Mark a hemline on the reverse side on all four edges, fold the raw edges on this line, and trim the corners diagonally to eliminate bulk. Glue the hem down with white all-purpose glue, then

press it firmly with a rolling pin or heavy bottle to flatten the hem and to distribute the glue evenly. After it is stencilled and hemmed, let the floor cloth dry for several days (so the colours won't bleed when varnished), then give it at least three coats of thinned varnish, making sure each coat has a chance to dry properly before applying the next. You can use polyurethane or acrylic varnish, but remember that several coats of the former – the more durable of the

two – will impart a yellowish tinge. If you want to give the floor cloth an aged appearance, add some raw umber to the first coat of varnish.

After it is finished, the floor cloth can be wiped clean with warm, soapy water. It may eventually need a fresh coat of varnish if cracks appear or if the varnish wears thin. Never fold the cloth, since this encourages cracking. If you need to move or store it, roll it loosely with the stencilled surface on the inside.

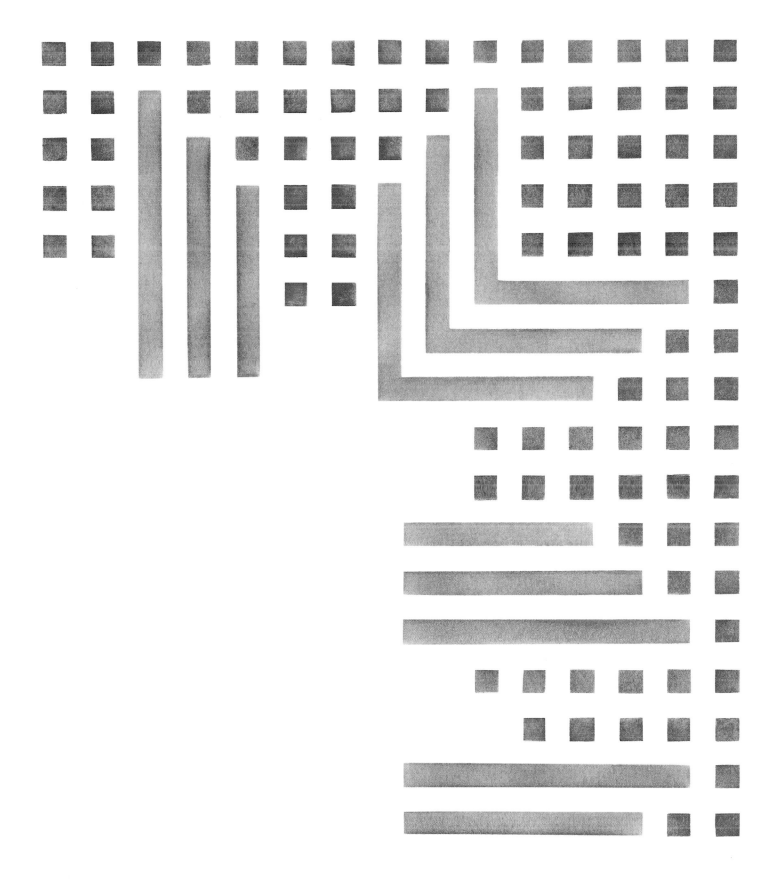

WALL PROJECTS

A master plan is also essential for very large projects, such as stencilling directly on a wall or a floor, although it will be easier to design a scaled-down version on graph paper than to arrange elements on the surface as you did with the floor cloth. After you decide where all the design elements are supposed to end up, cut the stencils, make paper proofs and satisfy yourself that the wall is at least clean, if not freshly painted (a flat finish is easiest to work on, but satin or eggshell is okay).

Now you have to mark up the wall so that you will know where to put the stencils. Use a chalk line if there is someone to help; otherwise, use a ruler and a soft pencil, chalk or small pieces of masking tape. (Be sure that whatever you use is removable.) With the ruler method, you don't need to mark solid, continuous lines. Small dashes or dots at intervals appropriate to the length of the stencil will do—just enough to give you a workable guideline. Remember, this line will coincide with the guideline on the stencil, not with the edge of the stencil itself, so measure accordingly.

Realize also that walls are seldom perfectly vertical, floors and ceilings hardly ever horizontal and corners rarely square. This is especially true of old houses. (The farmhouse we once lived in had a kitchen floor with such a pronounced slope that I had to start washing the floor in the northwest corner so that I would be mopping in the same direction the water was flowing.) As far as your guidelines are concerned, this means that you need to make a careful trade-off between true horizontal and vertical and the visual references in the room. For example, you do not want a horizontal border near a sloping ceiling or a vertical border near an off-kilter corner.

For simple repeating borders —probably the most common stencilled decoration for walls— one guideline is usually all you need. Just start at one end and keep going, repeat after repeat. When you get back to where you started, the end of the border will likely not match up exactly with the beginning. (This is a good reason for starting the border in an inconspicuous place.) Sometimes you can adjust the spacing between the last few prints to balance the alignment. Otherwise, try to fill the gap between the first and last prints with selected parts of the stencil so that the two blend seamlessly. I find the easiest way to turn a corner on a wall is to use another stencil cut out of Mactac. It is flexible enough to fit snugly into the corner, and its adhesive backing holds it there nicely. For more complex designs where the exact placement of each repeat is important, mark each stencil position on the guideline using the master plan as a guide.

The next step is to start stencilling. If you are nervous, start behind a door or a bookcase where mistakes will be less obvi-

ous. If there is carpet underfoot, move it or make sure it is well protected. Assemble all your supplies on a tray or cookie sheet so that they can be moved around easily. If you are working above floor level, put the cookie sheet on a wheeled trolley to save yourself a lot of bending. Tape the first stencil in place and paint; lift it, reposition and paint. It is more efficient to do all the repeats of one colour or one stencil first—for example, all the leaves or all the flowers—as there is less chance of getting mixed up or using the wrong colour or of paint building up on the stencils. Sometimes I'm willing to put up with the extra hassle of doing two colours at a time because I'm so eager to see the finished design, but I do not

recommend this approach for beginners—despite my years of experience, my overeagerness still leads me to make mistakes. Some stencillers like to use a one-piece stencil and allow adjacent colours to intermingle across the bridges. In this case, work with all colours at the same time.

The only thing different about stencilling an overall pattern—one that covers the whole surface instead of being confined to a border—is that the measuring is more complicated; you need to measure and mark a grid on the wall instead of a straight line. You will minimize the number of grids you have to measure and the number of times you have to reposition the stencil if you use a large stencil that includes several repeats.

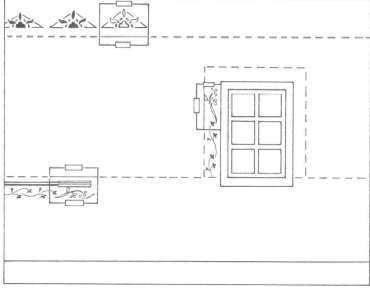

DOORS

Because doors form part of wall surfaces, this is probably the best place to say something about them. Panelled doors almost seem to invite some kind of decoration, and they certainly do not require as much preparation as walls do. Pick a design that looks as though it belongs in a rectangle, not something that looks like a border chopped off to fit a door. Adjust the size and placement of the design so that it is balanced in the space. Don't forget that it is best to work on a nonglossy finish. Some people like glossy woodwork, though. If this is the case, you will have to add an overcoat of glossy varnish later. Just to see if it could be done, I once stencilled teddy bears on a glossy door in my son's bedroom. I gave the door a fresh coat of semigloss paint the day before and used japan paints for the stencil work. I found that a circular brush motion moved paint around on the glossy surface but did not necessarily leave it where I wanted it. Stippling worked better, leaving tiny bristle dots of paint sitting on the surface, but if I reworked an area too much, it ended up blotchy because the bristles started picking up paint from the surface as well as depositing it. The final result was fairly satisfactory, but it would have been easier to work on a background with a duller texture.

FAKE TILES

Ambitious trompe-l'oeil projects are beyond the scope of the average do-it-yourselfer, but with the help of stencils, you can achieve surprising effects. One of these is fake tiles, which you create by stencilling traditional tile patterns on a suitably coloured background. Use a greyish felt pen to add grout lines between the "tiles," and finish with a coat of polyurethane to give the effect of a glazed sheen.

First, draw up a master plan on graph paper, showing the dimensions of the space and indicating tile placement (including any "cut" tiles). Refer to books or magazines for inspiration. Remember that some of the tiles can be plain ones, that you can have border tiles and that different arrangements of a single tile pattern can yield secondary patterns where the corners meet.

You need a smooth surface to begin with. To get a clean edge around your "tiled" space, mask it off from its surroundings with strips of masking tape. Paint the area to be decorated with two coats of flat (latex or alkyd) paint in the background colour. With the master plan as a guide, lightly mark a reference grid on the wall to show you where each fake tile will go. Use a sharp pencil and a set square for accuracy. Stencil the designs with a circular motion and a minimum of shading. Now take a warm grey felt pen, and remaining as relaxed as possible, draw freehand grout lines over the pencilled grid lines. Draw toward yourself, resting your baby finger against the wall for support and greater control. If the thought of doing anything freehand makes you tense, then use a ruler to guide the pen. If you need to use a ruler but don't want perfectly straight lines, a piece of wood will produce a less rigid effect. You can also use the pen to make tile corners look slightly rounded. Examine some real tiles to see how they look.

Let everything dry for two or three days before "glazing" with a coat of polyurethane. If the grouting shows any tendency to run (test the marker in an inconspicuous spot), then give it a coat of spray varnish first, use an acrylic varnish or coat it with shellac before applying the varnish. The same method can be used to create stencilled tile floors and tabletops.

ARCHITECTURAL DETAILS

You can also use stencils to create fake architectural details: cornice mouldings, chair rails, ersatz wall panelling or a frieze outline. This is the simplest kind of trompe-l'oeil, and it is very easy to do. You will be surprised at how you can create an illusion of carved or moulded plaster with just a touch of paint. All it takes is close attention to shading. Cut stencils of moulding details, then colour them in a monochrome fashion with different shades of the same colour. With an illustration from this book or a photograph of an actual moulding as a model, paint some parts of the design flat and shade others to suggest roundness or shadow according to the instructions outlined on page 47.

MURALS

A mural or landscape is not likely to be one of the first projects you stencil, but once you get hooked, it will probably not be long before you want to try one, even if it is only painted on the basement stairwell. The top photograph shows a mural I painted in the entry of my house, a rustic contrast to the formal murals in Schloss Laxenburg, below. So under the classification of "you never know when it might come in handy," I am including a brief summary of the method of painting stencilled landscape murals promoted by Rufus Porter in 1845. For more detailed instructions, read Porter's article, "The Art of Painting" (listed in Sources).

The first step is to establish the framework of the mural. According to Porter, the lower boundary should be on a line level with the bottom of the window—the dado line. The horizon line is four or five feet above the floor, and the upper boundary is the ceiling. For the large background parts of murals—land, water and sky—I buy ordinary white flat latex wall paint and add universal tinting colours (sold in any paint store) to create my own shades, although I buy very dark colours ready-mixed. For foreground details, I use either japan paints or acrylics. If the colours seem too bright, tone them down by adding some raw umber.

Begin by painting the background colour from the dado line to the horizon line, then paint the sky blue from the top of the wall down to about 10 inches above the horizon line. Paint this 10-inch gap with a cloud colour, blending the interface of the white and the blue while the paints are still wet. Work quickly because latex paint dries quite fast. Paint clouds (rising from the horizon or floating in the sky) by stippling with cloud colour before the blue paint is dry. Paint the lower edges of the clouds with a light slate colour and tip them with faint red or pink.

Outline the landscape design on the wall with a fine brush and diluted sky-blue paint. Include hills or mountains, cascades of water or farm scenes. Small spaces between windows and corners can be filled up with trees and shrubbery rising from the foreground.

To achieve an effect of depth, Porter divided the space between the dado line and the horizon line into several "distances," each characterized by a progressively smaller scale. In the foreground, trees should be three to six feet high and other objects sized proportionately. The second "distance" had trees 6 to 12 inches high and contained scenes of sporting or military activity. As one proceeds to the horizon, details are obscured and colours are dimmed with the addition of increasing amounts of sky blue until the farthest objects are nothing more than shaded blue outlines. Towns or cities in the distance can be represented by a few touches of the brush or pencil in pale colours.

Porter recommended using stencils to speed up the painting of houses, arbours, villages and so on. A house, for example, might need four stencils, one for the front, one for the side, one for the roof and a fourth for the windows. Although he did not suggest it, you could also use leaf stencils to help with foliage in the extreme foreground and single-edged stencils to produce waves in the background. In general, use stencils without details for distant objects, but add details to identifiable forms in the foreground.

FLOOR PROJECTS

In general, floors are even more work than walls. There are two things in particular that I find hard: measuring and being on my hands and knees for extended periods of time. The measuring is difficult because it has to be done in two dimensions over the whole surface. It is not at all like preparing a wall for a border, where all you have to do is snap a single chalk line. Even with an overall wall pattern, where the measuring is similar to that needed for floors, you at least have the advantage of being able to stand up while you do it.

After stencilling my first floor, I vowed I would never do another. Full of a beginner's enthusiasm and ignorance, I began drafting an elaborate design that would cover almost every inch of the floor. When the moment came to actually start putting paint on that large expanse of freshly—and expensively—sanded floor, I chickened out. It did not help that my husband was having fits at the prospect of my covering up all that lovely wood. I finally settled on a much more modest design—a border around the edge of the room and small floral sprigs placed at regular intervals over the rest of the floor. "A piece of cake," I thought to myself, not completely recognizing the significance of the word "regular." It all worked out very nicely on graph paper. Wide border around the edge, no sweat. Sprigs in a diamond pattern arranged symmetrically within the border—that took a bit of fiddling. It really helps in such circumstances to have a calculator handy and to work in metric units so that every measurement is a nice clean tenth of something, rather than a mixture of feet, inches and a half of three-eighths.

The next step was to transfer the measurements to the floor, a classic example of "easier said than done." Before starting, I put a coat of nonglossy varnish over the raw wood to protect it from any mistakes: the varnish would prevent paint from seeping indelibly into the wood grain. Having marked off the border around the room, I started at one end of the floor to mark the sprig positions. I measured the intervals very carefully and used a chalk pencil to make tiny dots where each sprig should go. By the time I got to the other end of the room, I had half-sprigs running into the border, which was not at all what I had planned. So I remeasured. It still didn't work.

Next I changed the scale of my drawing so that the intervals were different. This time, the last few rows of sprigs were not parallel to the border. I tried measuring from the side of the room instead of the end. By now, the floor was a mess of little dots, so I switched to using little squares of masking tape. In the end, I resorted to eyeballing, moving the bits of tape around until the whole thing looked more or less balanced. Since the sprigs were not connected to one another, such fudging worked out all right. In any case, once the room was finished, the furniture broke things up enough that no one could tell there was anything wrong with the spacing.

Measuring contributes the mental anguish to floor stencilling; working on your hands

and knees provides the physical punishment. The job always takes much longer than you think it will. It is sweaty, tiring work, and your knees and back will suffer no matter how fit you are. I started using a small cushion to kneel on, but it meant one more thing to move every time I shifted position, and if I wasn't careful, it would smudge the paint or knock something over. I ended up taping pieces of dense foam rubber to my knees; gardener's knee pads also work. There is nothing you can do for your back except stand up and stretch once in a while.

Of course, stencilling a floor does not have to be grim. If you start with a modest project such as this brick design and learn from my mistakes, it could even be fun. The most important part is the planning and measuring; the more effort you put into those preliminaries, the fewer problems you will have. Start with a small informal room, and

just do a simple border without bothering to refinish the floor first. (You should still lightly sand the border area and varnish it afterward to protect the stencilling.)

Or do as I once did—create a fake rug on a small part of the floor. In my case, the "rug" was designed to save me from having to get the whole floor refinished. One of the main traffic pathways in our house goes straight through part of the living room, and the strip of oak flooring along the thoroughfare had become quite worn and scuffed. The proper solution was to have the whole floor sanded and refinished, which would have been expensive, not to mention inconvenient, and I could not face moving all the furniture out of the room. As a temporary solution—one that will probably remain as long as we live here—I painted and stencilled a fake runner carpet over the offending part of the floor.

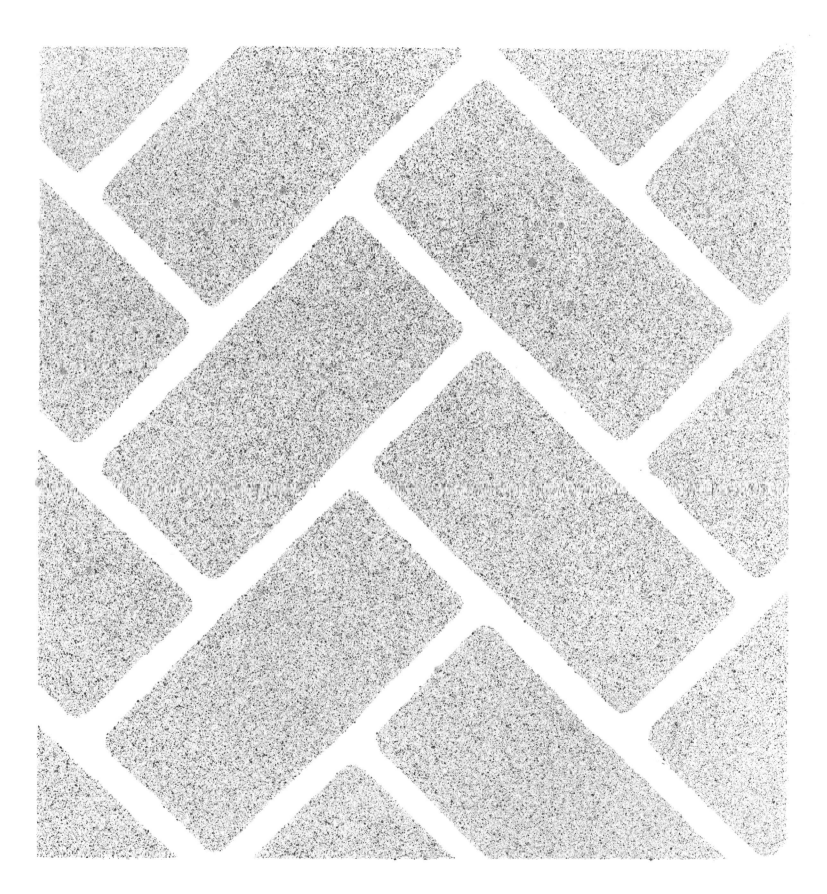

Before being stencilled, a floor can be bleached, painted with a few coats of flat oil-based paint or stained with an oil-based stain. If I am not using a painted background, I like to put on one coat of matte varnish first to give the floor a layer of protection and make it easier to correct mistakes. After the floor is stencilled, it has to be varnished to protect the paint, and unfortunately, the perfectly clear acrylic latex varnishes are not tough enough for the job. Polyurethane varnishes provide the greatest protection, but they impart a slightly yellow tinge to whatever they cover. For very dark colours, it probably won't matter much, but for lighter hues, you may want to take the yellowing into consideration when you choose your palette.

One final caveat: the fussier you are about a clean floor, the better the stencil job will be. Before you begin, you must thoroughly sweep, vacuum and dust with a tack cloth. But even so, little particles will land on the floor before you can paint it; there is no way you can totally eliminate them. I usually keep a tack cloth handy and use it to give each small section of floor a fresh wipe just before stencilling. When it comes to varnishing, though, particles will continue to appear while the varnish is drying, making it impossible to achieve an absolutely flawless surface. But as long as you have been reasonably thorough with your cleaning, they will be visible only to those who inspect the floor on their hands and knees.

As with overall wall patterns, a good master plan is essential for floor stencilling. Measure the room, and draw the outline of

the floor to scale on graph paper. Unless you are painting a checkerboard design, it will not matter if the floor is not perfectly square. Choose the pattern interval or block size for your stencil pattern, reduce it to the scale of the graph paper, and starting from the middle of the floor plan, mark the design intervals on it. Unless you are very lucky, there will be no way to fit a whole number of complete pattern blocks on both the length and the width of the floor. But by adjusting the size of the intervals and making judicious use of a border, you will be able to begin and end with complete patterns in at least one of the two directions. The pattern should be centred in both directions so that it will be symmetrical; then, wherever you have an incomplete block of the pattern, there will be the same fraction— half a diamond, for instance— on both edges.

Now you must transfer the grid and the master plan of the design to the floor. If you can rope someone in to help you, the task will be less likely to drive you crazy. And I do mean crazy, because if you cannot use a chalk line, you will have to use the longest straight edge you can find, take many more measurements and use a set square to keep your lines at right angles to one another. Stencilling on wood-plank or parquet flooring eliminates some of the headache of measuring, as the joints in the floor can be used to create all or part of the grid.

The first step in transferring the measurements is to find the exact centre of the floor. Do this by marking the centres of two opposite walls and snapping

a chalk line between them. If the room is a rectangle, you can also find the centre by snapping two diagonal chalk lines from the corners; the centre is where the diagonals intersect. The diagonals will come in handy later for checking the squareness of the grid.

Measure and mark the pattern intervals along the centre line (C), starting from the middle of the line and working out to the walls. The last interval marks at either end of the centre line will be close to the walls. Draw a line parallel to one of these walls that passes through the last interval mark. Now draw a line parallel to the opposite wall that passes through the last interval mark on that side of the room. If the room is a true rectangle, these two lines (A and B) should be parallel to each other and perpendicular to the centre line.

The next step is to measure the intervals in the other direction, across the room. Mark these intervals along the two lines that you have just drawn at either end of the room. Again, start at the centre of each line and work toward the walls. Now you have a line at each end of the room, both of them with points marking the pattern intervals. Join the corresponding points by drawing lines across the length of the room to form a set of parallel lines, the long lines of your grid.

All you need now are the cross lines of the grid, the spacing for which is already marked on the centre line. Mark the pattern intervals on one of the outer lines parallel to the centre line (D), and join the two sets of marks. The resulting grid allows you to position the stencils perfectly and easily, even if they

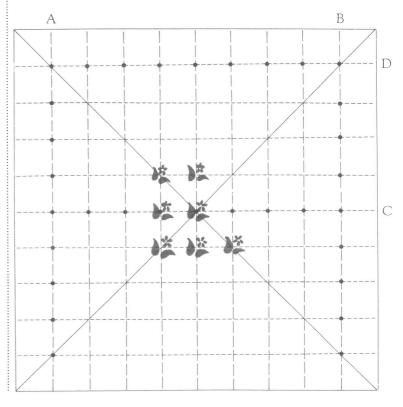

are opaque. One final caution before you begin: make sure that the registration system on the stencils corresponds to the grid as it is drawn on the floor.

Because floors are often decorated with larger designs than are walls, you may have to use heavier stencil material to give the stencils enough strength. You should use the largest stencil brush you can find. A roller will work too, as will spray paint, and will cover the area faster, but the prints will not be quite as crisp; the difference is hardly noticeable from standing height, however, and friends will not likely get down on hands and knees to examine each print.

Starting in one corner, stencil the borders. Turn corners by mitring, piecing or using a separate stencil (this should have been worked out beforehand on your master plan). Now fill in

the rest of the floor with the first of the stencils that make up the overall design, starting from the centre and working toward the edges. To lessen the chance of smudging, do every other grid in a row, then go back and fill in the ones between. If the motifs next to the border are not complete, first mask off the border with wide masking tape or newspaper taped in place. If the design requires more than one stencil, do the entire floor with one, start over with the second, and so on, until the design is complete.

Let everything dry for several days, then dust the floor with a tack cloth or vacuum cleaner. Apply varnish to a small area behind the door to make sure there is no bleeding. Then apply at least two coats of varnish to the whole floor according to the manufacturer's directions.

FURNITURE PROJECTS

It was a long time before I tried my hand at stencilling furniture. Most of our furniture seems to fall into two categories (mainly the second)—good and expensive or cheap and beat-up. Items belonging to the first category I was afraid of ruining, and items in the second category required so much preparatory work—repairing, sanding, stripping, priming, repainting and so on—that I was loath to undertake all the busywork just to get to the fun part of stencilling.

In the end, my 4-year-old son William forced my hand. The solid maple table in our kitchen had been reduced to a dismal state after seven years of abuse, and I set about restoring it by carefully sanding down to bare wood. At about the same time, William decided to change his middle name from Jonathan to Hot Rod. Then, in much the same way as an adult establishes a name change with a paragraph in the newspaper, William began making his name change official by writing "William Hot Rod Walters" in various and sundry places, including, to my horror, the freshly sanded tabletop. "William Hot Rod," spelled out in juicy magenta marker, had soaked right into the bare wood. There was little hope of sanding it out, so I had to paint over it, and having done that, there was no reason not to try a tabletop stencil.

What sort of furniture makes a good candidate for stencilling, and what does not? Painted decoration has always been used to disguise pieces of lesser quality, and that still holds true. You should not decorate valuable antiques or anything made of fine wood such as cherry or mahogany, but garage-sale bargains, hand-me-downs and survivors of student and young family days are all ideal candidates for stencil experiments. New but relatively inexpensive mass-produced furniture is also suitable, and since it is usually sold unassembled, you can put each part of it flat on a work table for stencilling, rather than having to crawl around on your hands and knees trying to work sideways and upside down.

Furniture has to stand up to a lot of wear and tear, so it is important to prepare the piece well. That means sanding old paint smooth—or stripping the finish if it is in really bad condition—priming bare wood, filling and sealing defects with shellac, then painting on an undercoat and several top coats, rubbing the surface smooth with sandpaper or steel wool between coats. Many thin coats of paint or varnish will give a much better finish than a few thick coats, and you should use oil-based or alkyd paints with a flat or non-glossy finish. The new latex flat enamels are also durable and can be used for furniture. At this point, you are ready to stencil, but you can seal the surface with a layer of varnish first if you like—to make it easy to wipe off errors. All the preparation is boring and tedious, but the results make it worthwhile.

There is not much difference between stencilling a wall or a Christmas card and stencilling a piece of furniture. The biggest difference is in the design process, because you need a motif that is just the right size and is arranged in a pattern that complements the style and structure of the furniture. Keep the colour scheme simple, and rely on the pattern of the motifs for the decorative effect. Work out several possibilities on paper first, and if you need inspiration, look up some library books on folk art or painted furniture.

After the stencils are painted and have dried thoroughly, apply several thin coats of varnish to the finished work to protect the surface and to give it whatever degree of shine is appropriate. Remember that anything painted in an early-19th-century rural style should have a fairly matte finish.

CHAPTER FOUR

CHILDREN'S ROOMS

Stencilling for children can be wonderfully rewarding. This is your chance to let your imagination go without worrying about doing everything exactly right, because "right" in this case is producing a room that delights the child. Young children are the last ones to notice flaws in your technique or artistry, especially if the designs capture their current interests. I always tell my kids that "it's supposed to be that way" if they comment on some particularly blatant goof, and even if they don't agree with me completely, they will allow me some artistic licence.

This chapter is devoted to stencilling for kids and by kids; it is full of ideas for decorating their walls, floors and furniture, and it has a whole range of stencil designs to copy. Stencilling a child's room can involve as much or as little effort as you want, and it is cheaper and a lot more fun than wallpaper. You can paint a small border or an ambitious mural, trim the sheets, stencil a quilt, a lampshade, the furniture, switch plates, the floor—anything that is not too shiny.

Children tend to be more enthusiastic about things they have helped to create, so if you can bring yourself to accept somewhat less-than-perfect results (the size of the "somewhat" varies inversely with the age of the child), then let your children help with the stencilling. It goes without saying that you should supervise closely and be prepared to expend twice as much effort as you would without your little helpers. Before you start, protect the floor with a drop cloth and the children with aprons or smocks. For preschoolers, you should position the stencil and load the brush with paint; older children can do it themselves.

Using a sponge may be a better idea—you won't need to worry about brush technique, and imperfections will be less obvious. For this method, simply dip a well-wrung-out sponge into the paint, blot it on a paper towel to remove any excess and dab over the stencil. When stencilling with children, make sure you use nontoxic water-based paints—solid disc paints will do, or mix up a very thick paste of powdered paints. If you use paint that is not durable, you can protect it afterward with a coat of polyurethane. Just keep telling yourself that the whole objective is to make the occupants of the room happy, not to be on the cover of *House and Garden*.

Having said all that, I have to admit to being somewhat hypocritical: I could not bring myself to let my own children (they were 3 and 6 at the time) help paint their rooms. My first project for them involved converting a closet into an alcove for their

trundle bed. The inspiration for the painted decoration (I'm almost never spontaneously creative, but my sources of inspiration are varied) was an illustration of a set for an 1816 Berlin production of Mozart's *The Magic Flute*. It depicted the entrance to the Queen of the Night's palace, with a curved dome of stars set in a dark night sky and a new moon resting on a low bank of clouds. The Queen of the Night stood imposingly on the moon.

Well, my boys didn't think that much of the Queen; they wanted a Care Bear instead. While they fought over what *kind* of Care Bear, I painted the sky, stencilled the stars and sponged in the clouds. I did not really know how one was

supposed to do all that—I just bought a few cans of latex paint and started, hoping it would not end up being too awful.

Then I laboriously painted a freehand Birthday Bear with acrylic paint. I did it freehand because I did not know I could stencil it, and it was laborious because the boys supervised every last detail: "Mom, that's not quite the right yellow," "Mom, the tummy isn't round enough," and "Mom, the ears don't look like that, and the cupcake isn't in the right place." So, while they did not actually apply the paint themselves, they certainly did participate in the production.

Soon after that, they decided that if Mom got to paint pictures on the walls, it must be okay for them to paint pictures

on the walls too. The difference was that they used felt pens. The first time I spotted one of these creations, I thundered, "Who did that?" Three-year-old William strutted over to it, posed proudly and announced enthusiastically, "I did, Mom!"

One way of letting very young kids feel that they are participating is to cut them a few simple stencils and set them up at a table with coloured pencils and felt pens to make prints on paper. The pencils and pens work really well with stencils (as you may remember from your own kindergarten days). I now pass all my old stencils to the kids, and they have a lot of fun making paper prints, some of which end up as birthday wrapping paper and greeting cards.

STENCIL A CHILD'S BORDER, FACING
PAGE, A PLAY MAT, ABOVE, OR LET
THE KIDS FILL IN THEIR OWN STEN-
CILS USING FELT PEN, TOP RIGHT,
COLOURED PENCIL, RIGHT, AND
CRAYON, BELOW.

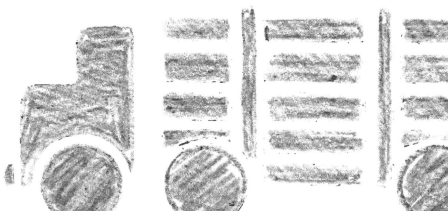

Children's design preferences change quickly. One year, they cannot live without teddy bears and balloons; the next year, it has to be trains or spaceships. With stencilled decoration, it is easy and inexpensive to change the look of a room to keep pace with their evolving interests. All it takes is a bit of paint and some elbow grease.

Before deciding on a design, try to imagine what the room looks like from your child's perspective. Don't bother with stencil work near the ceiling. Kids will never notice it, and besides, stencilling way up there is very hard on your neck. You need something at a level appropriate to the size of the person living there. This might mean a stencilled border at baseboard level for crawlers or one that is three feet off the ground for toddlers. Borders can also be applied at crib or bed height. In a baby's room, don't automatically put the wall border on a level with the top of the crib. Cribs are normally meant for sleeping, and you don't want your baby standing up to admire your handiwork every time he or she is put down for a nap. If you make the border just above the height of the mattress where it will be visible though the bars, then the baby might have one more inducement to lie down and go to sleep. Also, in another year or so when he or she graduates to a real bed, the border will still be at a good height— more or less at eyeball level— whether the child is in bed or up and playing.

There are a few things you can do to make redecorating easier. If you confine the stencilling to borders (they can be any width

BOTH THE BABY'S QUILT AND THE WALL BORDER, ABOVE, WERE CREATED USING A MONOCHROME BUTTERFLY STENCIL, FACING PAGE, THAT WAS ADAPTED FROM A JAPANESE TEXTILE DESIGN. THE BUTTERFLIES ON THE BLANKET ARE ENCLOSED BY THE DOUBLE-HELIX RIBBON PICTURED ON PAGES 98-99. IF THE HEIGHT OF THE BORDER IS CAREFULLY PLANNED, YOU CAN LATER PAINT OVER THE RIBBONS AND BUTTERFLIES WITH A WIDER BLUE BORDER AND STENCIL ON THE CONSTELLATIONS VISIBLE IN THE LOCAL NIGHT SKY.

you want), then as long as the rest of the walls can be spruced up with a good washing, you can simply redo the border without repainting the rest of the room. To restencil a border, place wide masking tape along its upper and lower edges. If you still have some of the old wall paint, seal the tape as described on page 31. Now pick a new background colour for the border. Don't use the same colour as the rest of the walls, because a new coat of paint will always look fresher.

Paint over the old stencils with this new background colour, completely filling the area between the strips of masking tape. You will need several coats to cover the old stencils properly. Carefully remove the masking tape. Let the background paint dry overnight, then stencil in the new border design.

You will have realized by now that this technique means your new border has to be at least as wide as the old one. It can be wider but not narrower. It also means that you cannot change the position of the border every year unless you want to repaint the whole room.

Because a babe in arms is unlikely to quibble over your choice of fabric and colour, the nursery is the one room of the house where you can ignore convention and indulge your fantasies. Go ahead and be outrageous. Your baby certainly will not complain, and you can give your creative itches a good scratch. Besides, many outrageous ideas result in final products that are not at all farfetched. The important thing is not to agonize over what to do—just get started. After all, we're only

talking about paint here. If you do not like the result, paint it out and start again. You will find that when you do not have to be too serious about what you are doing, you can have a lot of fun. Once past the age of 3 or 4, your children will likely take a more proprietary interest in anything you want to do to their rooms, and your artistic efforts will be severely censored if not vetoed outright. All the more reason to go a bit wild with nursery decorating before your wings are clipped.

The designs in this section were included specifically with babies and children in mind, but many designs elsewhere in the book would also be suitable. Don't feel you have to limit yourself to using these designs as they are. Modify them if you like, combine them with other motifs or arrange them into landscapes. Imagine a foot-wide border around the room or a two- or three-foot frieze positioned next to the baseboard. Consider doing something different with the background of wide borders—subtly changing pastels or fluffy white clouds on a blue sky, for example. Then enlarge the stencils to an ap-

propriate size on a photocopier and paint them over the background. Or if you find borders too confining, paint random flocks of birds or butterflies flying up one wall and down another or a garden of wildflowers growing around the edge of the room. Remember that you are not limited to walls alone. You can stencil on floors, toy boxes, furniture, bed linens, curtains; make quilts or duvet covers; decorate shirts, jackets, baby clothes. If your kids like playing with Lego, Brio or Playmobil, you can use stencils to help paint a village map on the floor.

BEARS

The secret to painting adorable teddy bears is to make them short and fat. I have included several different bears here, all of them short and fat. All use the same basic parts of the bear stencil, and you can change the clothes or use a different set of legs to make him stand instead of sit. Replace the ears and add whiskers to transform the bear into a rabbit.

In stencilling the bear, make sure you paint the body stencil quite light so that the facial details show up. The outside edges should be darker and the centre lighter to give an effect of roundness. Stitching and mouth details can be added later with felt pen, paintbrush or pencil crayon. The same bear can be stencilled without bridges as well, which means using a few more stencils to eliminate the gaps.

HEARTS

The heart is one of the basic folk-art motifs of most European countries, so it is not surprising to find it well represented in the decorative arts of North American settlers. The artisans of rural Quebec usually added a touch of carved decoration to their furniture and utensils, as did their predecessors in early-18th-century France, and elongated hearts can be found on wooden furniture, carved maple-sugar moulds, pewter spoons and wrought-iron trivets. Symbolizing both secular and religious love, as well as a host of other virtues, the heart became associated in folk art with traditions surrounding courtship, marriage and the founding of the family. Hearts adorned family records, bookplates, quilts, furniture, household utensils and textiles, as well as valentines and love tokens, and they came in many different shapes, some of them associated with particular cultures.

The heart stencils pictured here are all extremely easy to do. If you prefer one type of heart to another, simply substitute your favourite in any of the designs. You can also colour the heart uniformly without shading, or you can make the outside edge darker and the centre quite light. The heart can be made fancier with a border, as shown.

To do this, cut two heart stencils, one slightly larger than the other. Stencil the big one first with the colour you want for the border, then do the smaller one on top of the first and centred within it.

Pink and red are the most traditional heart colours today, but in the past, especially among the Pennsylvania Dutch, hearts were painted in just about every colour available. With a change in colour, hearts immediately lose their feminine look.

The Pennsylvania Dutch, who sometimes painted hearts black, often pictured tulips growing from a heart to symbolize the adage, "From a pure heart, good works develop." These motifs were usually painted freehand, but there is no reason why you cannot stencil them. Likewise, hearts were often combined with various forms of leaves, sometimes similar to the freehand decorative designs of the Germans and Swiss. You could make them even more similar by adding freehand accents. As the variations on a heart-shaped border illustrate, it is a good idea to fiddle with a basic motif that you like instead of just copying it as is. You might come up with something that you like even better, and you will have the added satisfaction of making it a bit more original.

FLOWERS

The stylized flower-bud border on the right was one of my first designs and is one that everyone seems to like. Shown in the photograph on page 64 as a stencilled pillow, this border is a very easy one for the beginning stenciller. It uses one stencil for each colour and has no shading, and the registration need not be terribly accurate. The cutting doesn't have to be perfect either. Don't worry if the curves look more like sections of straight lines strung together. The final print will still be wonderful. Because this design has very small cutouts and relatively large bridges, the stencil does not have to be really strong, so if you have trouble cutting it, try using Mac Tac or heavy waxed paper instead of Mylar. Reduce the stickiness of the Mac Tac by sticking it to your clothes and lifting it off a few times. You'll find the residual tack makes stencilling onto fabric easier, as it holds the stencil in place and stops the fabric from shifting.

Our garden has masses of periwinkle growing in the shade of azaleas and rosebushes, and couldn't resist designing a border of these little blue blossoms with the evergreen leaves. The border, on the far right, is also an easy one, although it takes three stencils. The centre ribs on the leaves are too narrow to hold up as bridges on a single green stencil, so I cut one stencil for stems and lower leaf halves and a second stencil for upper leaf halves. Both the rosebud and the periwinkle borders can be reduced in size and used to create very pretty borders on stationery, birth announcements, baby pillows — anything small.

94

LACE

Like ribbons and flowers, lace is often associated with feminine things and baby clothes. Simulating real lace with stencils involves an incredible amount of finicky cutting to create the stencil. I find the easiest way is to paint the background rather than the white part. However, you can achieve a very believable impression of lace with stencils modelled after cotton eyelet or embroidered cutwork and painted in a very delicate colour over a white or off-white background. Or for something more akin to a trompe-l'oeil effect, stencil with white on a darker background, then give the whole "fabric" part a thin coat of transparent white glaze, which makes it look like white embroidery on an almost sheer white fabric.

RIBBONS AND BOWS

Ribbon bows and swags— whether carved, moulded or painted—were frequently used in European decoration during the last few centuries, nowhere more so than in 18th-century upper-class French bedchambers. Ever since then, ribbons, ruffles and roses have been a recurring romantic motif for wallpapers and fabrics. I have included a variety of ribbon stencils in this chapter, but they do not have to be reserved exclusively for nursery decorations.

Most of them would be suitable for any bedroom decorated in a romantic style—on walls, bed linens or painted furniture. In miniature, they are also suitable for stationery. The important thing is to use a size of bow that is proportionate to whatever is being decorated. Bows that look perfect on the printed page could be used as is on small things such as cards and quilts, but at that size, they would disappear if stencilled onto a wall. Experiment a bit with a photo-

copier, and make paper proofs in various sizes before beginning the actual project.

One of the ribbon stencils was inspired by a photograph of a painted bedroom border in the house of early-20th-century Swedish illustrator Carl Larsson. I believe you can now buy wallpaper copies of Larsson's hand-painted design, but why would you want to buy wallpaper when you can stencil your own version? Ribbon patterns illustrate the versatility of stencil-

ling, for they allow you to adjust the length of the swags (and hence the distance between bows) so that you do not end up with one-third of a swag when you finish the room.

Add a simple bouquet to one of the bows, and you have a matching motif for the front of a drawer, the back of a chair or a door panel. The double-helix ribbon border with no bows can be used to elegantly frame pictures, mirrors, furniture doors and fake wall panels.

SCENIC BORDERS

It is easy to get hooked on scenic borders. Part of the appeal lies in knowing that you are doing something quite unique, and part is in the excitement of watching the composition unfold beneath your brush.

Scenic stencilling is more complex than simple borders. In the photographed example, I used latex paint and ordinary brushes first to paint the sky, then to stipple on the clouds. (With a white wall, you could use cloud-shaped Mylar to cover the cloud parts and paint the rest of the wall blue.) Using masking tape for a straight edge, I added the grass, again in latex paint. Finally, I stencilled the fence, then the sheep and the flowers.

If you want to paint a sheep

with sky as the background, the animal should be either a dark colour or some colour that will still look all right with blue showing through—blue, green, purple or pink, for example, unless the paint is opaque. I used opaque acrylics for the sheep so that I did not have to worry about the background colour. The body of each sheep was shaded and stippled coarsely to make it look fluffy.

I also used acrylics for the fence and flowers, which I painted against the light sky and clouds. You need opaque paint to put the flowers over the grass. If the grass is too dark or the flowers too light, stencil the flowers in white before doing their final colour.

SUNBONNET SUE

Originally an appliqué quilt design, Sunbonnet Sue has been around for a long time. Here, I have made up three variations in stencil format and put them in a simple border edged with checks. You could turn this into a more elaborate scenic border with clouds, flowerbeds, farm animals and trees.

BOATS

Nautical themes are popular with young and old alike and can be used to decorate a library or a recreation room as well as a nursery. There are big boats here, and little ones, but of course, you can alter the sizes to suit the application. One design is Canada's most famous sailing vessel, the *Bluenose* schooner. I have also included a little border of boats, my stencilled version of a few of the 16 different types of sailing vessels embossed on the bathroom window of our 60-year-old house. The rest of the sailboats come from a small 1913 Scottish stencil catalogue that I happened across while browsing in the depths of the University of British Columbia library. Notice the patterns used to fashion a border of waves at the bottom. Any of these designs could be paired with a fat rope border or embellished with some kind of wave stencil like the one on page 49.

DINOSAURS

Dinosaurs are enjoying an incredible wave of popularity; even the youngest child can pronounce the difficult names with ease. My sons not only insisted that I include dinosaur stencils in their room, but 7-year-old Daniel checked them for accuracy and made sure that I specified the geological age in which they lived. Two stencil styles are used for the animals— the simplest is done with one stencil and is the best one for children to use. The second version uses an extra stencil to eliminate the bridges and to give more definition to the legs.

HORSES

Until the invention of photography in the 18th century, no one knew how horses moved their legs when they ran; it happened too fast for the eye to pick out the pattern of movement. That is why artists used to portray galloping horses with both forelegs outstretched and hind legs extended in a sort of flying gallop. Then in 1878, Eadweard Muybridge captured the true sequence of action in a gallop by using a battery of cameras placed at regular intervals along a racetrack. The two rows of stencilled images below illustrate this entire sequence. They would make a good border for the bedroom of a "horsey" teenager. In subdued colours, an equestrian border would also be appropriate for a den or a study.

MUSIC

One last idea, this one for music lovers, is a border of music notation illuminated in the tradition, if not the exact style, of 17th- and 18th-century music books that were printed and decorated with stencils. Stencil the five staff lines or draw them freehand with a felt pen held firmly against a long straight edge, stencil the notes in the appropriate positions, and add some spontaneous floral stencilling for colour. If possible, pick a song that has special significance for your child.

CHAPTER FIVE

STENCIL STYLES

Decorative patterns are always more interesting to me when I know something about where they came from and how they were originally used. Sometimes their stories involve more than just an ornamental context, and I end up sidetracked into the history of baroque music or the tale of some 19th-century explorer, which more often than not inspires more ideas for new stencil designs and applications.

This chapter offers a brief look at decorative stencilling in Canada, its styles and influences. It is not by any means an exhaustive study but rather an introduction to the history of stencilling that will breathe life into traditional patterns. The range of stencil designs and applications over the past few centuries is remarkable, and the accompanying photographs and illustrations should enlarge your stencil repertoire. However, if you use these motifs, be sure to enlarge them, for some will lose their original boldness if reproduced as small as they appear in this book.

Canada has a rich tradition of interior decorative painting, which, like many things Canadian, reflects a number of different cultural styles and which, again like many things Canadian, has gone largely unheralded. By far the two strongest decorative influences were the immigrants who flooded into Canada from the United States in the late 18th and early 19th centuries and the styles that emanated from Victorian England throughout the last half of the 19th century. In the 20th century, art nouveau held sway for the first two decades until stencilling effectively died out. Since its rediscovery and revival in the 1970s, "country" has been the predominant stencil theme.

There used to be many fine examples of the various stencil styles in cities all across North America. Unfortunately, few remain. Photographic records of interiors are very scarce, often lacking in detail and certainly in colour. Houses that have been spared from destruction or renovation have generally been painted or repapered more than once since the end of the 1800s. Small, isolated towns, places without the big-city penchant for newness, have fared somewhat better in preserving the past. The small towns of Nova Scotia, for example, still harbour a rich treasury of uncorrupted and sometimes restored 19th-century houses, many with painted interior decoration still marvellously intact. That is where we look for inspiration today.

EARLY-19TH-CENTURY RURAL

The revival of popular interest in stencilling in the United States has been so closely and widely associated with early-American folk and decorative art that it is easy to overlook the fact that stencilling was not at all universal in 18th- and 19th-century America. Except for the decoration of furniture, stencilling was largely a rural phenomenon. Townspeople had access to imported fabrics and wallpapers that were too expensive for and often unavailable to settlers in the country, who relied, instead, on stencilling to decorate their walls and floors.

In Canada, there was little or no secular stencilling before the late 1700s. Although the French settlers used stencilling techniques to decorate church interiors, they had no tradition of using them to decorate their homes or furniture. The American Revolution, however, had an enormous impact on decorative customs because of the huge numbers of refugees—or Loyalists, as they were called—that poured north of the border in the 1780s, almost doubling the country's population overnight. The Loyalists came largely from the New England countryside, where the stencilling tradition was strong, and when they resettled in what later became Ontario and the Maritime Provinces, they brought their stencilling skills with them.

From surviving examples of stencilled floors, furniture and walls, it is obvious that the motifs and placement of patterns are virtually identical to those found in New England. Some of the work would have been done by the homeowner, but most was carried out by itinerant artists who worked in exchange for room and board or perhaps for a small fee.

The stencillers travelled from place to place, their saddlebags packed with stencils, brushes and small bags of powdered pigments. Clients would pick out the designs and colours they wanted from the painter's collection. Thus, along the route of each stenciller, one finds the same stencils used again and again but not always in the same combinations or colours. It was also quite common for a painter to copy stencils from the work of another or to borrow a design from a neighbour, so one finds numerous variations on each design theme, some more graceful or applied with greater skill than others.

The colours were bold and simple. If we tend to think of early North American decoration as being dull and muddy, it is probably because the stencils that still survive have faded over time. In Ontario, some examples of light, delicate stencilling over white, pink and pale blue backgrounds have been found under layers of wallpaper. Wall stencils were typically painted red, pink, green, yellow and black on plaster walls painted white, pink, yellow, grey, light green or light blue. Good manufactured paint was expensive, so paints were usually homemade according to recipes published in magazines and cookbooks. Colours were often derived from natural sources such as nicotine, charred potatoes or beets; the pigments were mixed in skimmed milk, whitewash or distemper (a mixture of whiting, glue sizing and water, which was sold commercially in Canada as Kalso-

mine). Sometimes walls were varnished as well.

In the 50 years that followed the American Revolution, the stencils in Upper Canada, New England and parts of the Maritimes all relied on the same basic motifs, most of which were simplified versions of designs from European folk decoration on pottery, porcelain, textiles, carved woodwork and wallpaper. The origins of many of the designs go back far beyond the colonies of North America or even 18th-century Europe. For example, a border of ivy—the symbol of friendship—was commonly used by the ancient Greeks to decorate vases, and it often reappears as a vine border in stencils of the early settlers. Imported wallpaper was a great source of inspiration, and although the stencilled motifs were simplified, they were arranged on the wall according to the best wallpaper conventions—borders, friezes, single motifs and overmantel designs. Walls left plain except for an outlining frieze and border would often have corners filled with quarter-fans.

Border designs were extremely popular. They outlined windows, mantels and doors. Sometimes a wall would be completely covered with vertical border designs. More often, the wall would be divided by vertical borders into panels decorated with single motifs that were fairly large, up to 12 inches across. Border motifs included stylized leaves and flowers and a wide variety of geometric forms; realistic designs were rare.

The tops of walls were usually edged with elaborate friezes six inches or more wide. In style,

the frieze often echoed 18th-century French fashion, with stencilled versions of swags and festoons, tassels and pendants. Frieze motifs also included sunbursts, arches, stylized leaf or flower borders, bells and geometric patterns. Sometimes the pattern would be edged with one or more geometric borders.

Single motifs were usually arranged in some sort of regular pattern over a wall, but they could also be incorporated into an overmantel design. These motifs included floral sprays, wreaths, sunbursts, pineapples, stylized leaves and a host of circular designs.

The most elaborate design of the room was placed over the mantel, painted either directly on the wall or on canvas or wood panels. The overmantel design usually consisted of eagles, peacocks, horsemen, weeping willows or bouquets of flowers in baskets or urns. Sometimes the flower arrangement was made by stencilling several overlapping repeats of a flower spray used elsewhere on the wall, without any regard for the direction of curvature of the stems. In other cases, flowers were grouped as if they really did belong in the container.

The stencilling of patterns on walls reached the height of its popularity in the first quarter of the 19th century; by 1850, wallpaper was cheap enough that it replaced any need for stencilling and it was used in almost every room in the house. Meanwhile, the French were manufacturing sets of scenic wallpaper that were used to create room-sized murals. With typical 19th-century flamboyance, the murals featured exotic themes such as Captain Cook's voyage around the world, natives of the Pacific and *The Reconciliation of Venus and Psyche*. What was good enough for the French was usually good enough for the colonists, and around 1825, several New England artists, inspired by the wallpapers, began to popularize the painting of scenic murals directly onto plaster walls. Foremost among these artists was the inventor, jack-of-all-trades and future founding editor of *Scientific American*, Rufus

Porter. After watching itinerant stencillers ply their craft, he had the idea of using stencils to make murals faster and easier to paint. So convinced was he that he had developed a technique that would enable a do-it-yourselfer to produce personalized murals that he included a thorough description of his methods in the first volume of *Scientific American* in 1845 (see Sources). Nova Scotians must have been quite partial to this type of decoration, for there are many surviving examples in that province and the practice of mural painting never died out there as it did elsewhere.

Early Canadian settlers stencilled more than their walls. Floor cloths made of heavy coated sailcloth, painted in patterns and nailed down to cover the entire floor, added decoration underfoot and also stopped drafts from coming through the floorboards. Floor cloths reached the peak of their popularity in the last half of the 18th century. Although few examples of stencilled floors have survived in Canada, where they were considered an American custom, they were probably just as common as in the northern United States, since both stencilled floors and floor cloths are evident in the backgrounds of contemporary portraits.

Early floor cloths—those from the 17th century—were painted in bold geometric designs resembling tiles, usually black and white and sometimes marbleized. Over the next 100 years, designs became more elaborate and more colourful and were often adapted from earlier English ornamentation. By the 19th century, the patterns were stencilled instead of painted freehand. The rich could buy imported floor cloths or commission European artists to create them tailormade for particular rooms. Manufactured and printed oilcloths were available in the 1840s but were too expensive for the average homemaker, who, following instructions available in magazines and books, could substitute homemade floor cloths fashioned from canvas, sailcloth or even heavy brown paper. The paper ones were made by gluing small pieces together, sizing and oiling the sheet, then painting geometric patterns and adding freehand or stencilled borders. A smaller version of the floor cloth, and one that was uniquely Maritime, was the sailcloth mat, traditionally used on Grand Banks fishing schooners as a sort of bedside floor mat placed under a sleeping hammock or next to a bunk.

In the late 1700s, in both Canada and the United States, itinerant decorators began to stencil designs directly onto floors to imitate and substitute for the more expensive rugs and floor cloths. Typically, one or more large, bold motifs would be stencilled over the entire surface in a repeat pattern, with a running border about a foot wide around the edge. Background colours were grey, yellow ochre, dark green or brown, and the patterns were stencilled in black, white, yellow, green, grey or dark red.

Stencilled floor cloths and floors were gradually replaced by cheaper machine-produced floor coverings in the second half of the 19th century, although floor coverings of any sort were still a luxury in most of Canada. At about the same time, rural women started making hooked rugs, which became very popular because they provided a means of converting worn-out hand-me-down clothing into warm floor coverings. The rugs were not stencilled, but the colours of the fabric strips could be arranged in various designs, and it was not long before a tin peddler in Maine discovered that he could make templates out of zinc, use the templates to mass-produce stencilled patterns on burlap and sell the burlap to housewives for rug hooking. Soon entrepreneurs in Montreal and the Maritimes followed suit with their own "paint-by-number" rug-hooking patterns. One of the better-known patterns from a Nova Scotia company was of the *Bluenose*.

Except for the odd chair back or cradle, stencilled decoration was not commonly applied to early Canadian country furniture. The Germanic communities had a tradition of painted decoration and apparently stencilled not only walls but also farm wagons and children's sleighs, although to a lesser degree in Canada than in the United States. Objects such as containers, chests and game boards were often decorated with painted designs, sometimes freehand, sometimes stencilled.

French-Canadian country furniture was generally characterized by carved rather than painted ornamentation. There are a few examples of Indian ash-splint baskets with coloured decoration, which, although stampprinted, has the same structure as stencil motifs.

It was more common to find stencilled decoration on fancier styles of furniture, especially chairs. The stencilling was done with metallic powders in ornate patterns in an attempt to imitate the elaborate ormolu and inlaid metal decoration characteristic of the Empire and Directoire furnishings fashionable in Europe and urban North America in the early 19th century. This particular type of stencilled decoration developed first in the

ALTHOUGH CANADIAN FURNITURE
HAS TRADITIONALLY BEEN EN-
HANCED WITH CARVED RATHER
THAN PAINTED DECORATION,
CHAIR BACKS WERE SOMETIMES
STENCILLED IN BRONZE, GOLD
OR SILVER METALLIC POWDERS,
RIGHT, TO IMITATE THE ELABO-
RATE ORMOLU AND INLAID PAT-
TERNS OF EUROPEAN EMPIRE AND
DIRECTOIRE FURNISHINGS. DELI-
CATELY SHADED OVER DARK
WOOD, THE MOTIFS WERE LARGELY
CLASSICAL. LEAVES, BELOW, AND
BASKETS OF FRUIT, FACING PAGE,
WERE ESPECIALLY POPULAR.

United States, where cabinet-makers, lacking craftsmen experienced in decorative metalwork, found a substitute in the technique of stencilling with gold, silver and bronze powders.

This stencilling with metallic powders had already been perfected when Europeans tried to copy oriental lacquer ware, but its use on furniture in America led to the development of a unique style, one that showed, at least in the beginning, a very high level of workmanship. The designs, on early pieces especially, are elaborate, delicate and detailed. Unlike country wall and floor stencilling of the time, the gold stencil work on furniture was delicately shaded (usually over dark wood) so that the wood grain showed through

the more transparent parts.

The motifs were largely classical—acanthus leaves, Greek honeysuckle, fruit and flowers. Miniature landscapes and collections of seashells were stencilled onto chair backs. As the demand for such furniture grew, it began to be mass-produced, the stencilled designs becoming simpler so that the finished pieces could be cranked out as fast as they were assembled.

The leaf was probably the most popular of the motifs, the acanthus the most popular of all, especially for formally decorated furniture. The acanthus, which grows wild in southern Europe, was first adopted as an ornamental motif by the Greeks. Since then, it has recurred in every Western style,

although it has never acquired any symbolic significance. As depicted in 19th-century stencils, the acanthus was always stylized, although other leaves, such as oak and maple, were rendered in naturalistic forms. Whatever the form, leaves were used as background for flower and fruit arrangements and as borders on chairs, clocks, wardrobes, trays, mirrors and boxes. One of the most common types of border was formed of overlapping leaves, much like the one described on page 47. I rather like leaves stencilled without veins, although to be properly representative of the style of the day, they should have them.

Another common motif for furniture was a basket or vase of fruits, leaves and flowers.

Each item would usually be a separate stencil. The items were assembled piece by piece, with paper to mask off whatever one didn't want painted. Leaves were used to fill up the background. The exercise on page 50 shows you how to construct such a grouping.

Sometime after 1815, plain factory-woven cotton cloth became available and was used to make counterpanes—bed covers intended for decoration rather than warmth. Once again, stencilling was put to use. The counterpanes were block printed or stencilled by hand in simple designs in red, green and yellow that imitated the appliquéd quilts and elaborately embroidered bedspreads popular at the time.

VICTORIAN

With the Loyalists came a marked American influence on rural stencil styles in the early 1800s. But just as strong was the influence of England, particularly during the latter half of the century when Victoria reigned over Britain's golden age. The Victorian era in England was a time of incredible technological and social change, the transition to the industrial age. Its impact was felt in the colonies, not only through the traditions transplanted with British immigrants but also through the British publications that dominated the North American market.

Although hardly a fashionable figure herself, Queen Victoria had considerable influence on styles because she was a popular monarch and people sought to emulate her. For example, on her first visit to Scotland, as a tactful gesture, the Queen wore an outfit made of tartan cloth. When her portrait was painted in this attire, scarlet plaids became the fashion on both sides of the Atlantic. The Victorians began to use tartans even more lavishly after Prince Albert decorated the interior—including carpets, draperies and upholstery—of Balmoral Castle exclusively in tartans. Because Victoria reigned for such a large part of the 19th century, her name has become synonymous with the highly embellished styles characteristic of those years.

Decoration was taken very seriously by the Victorians, and what may seem like haphazard clutter to us was, in fact, a careful combination of patterns and colours that followed certain well-established rules while still leaving room for individual creative expression. To appreciate the Victorian style, one has to know a little about the times. Several factors were to play important roles—directly or indirectly—in determining the decorative styles of the century.

One was the writing of Sir Walter Scott, who popularized Gothic romances, lavish recreations of chivalry in mediaeval times. Gothic became the fashion in architecture, furniture, fabrics, wallpapers, painted decoration and illustration. If Scott liked stone castles, black oak and rich colours, then by golly, the Victorians would decorate their houses, no matter how humble, with crimson wallpaper and painted simulations of marble, stone and dark wood, as well as painted and stencilled friezes of mediaeval design. The works of Lord Byron, who typified the romantic ideals of the 19th century, were just as popular as those of Scott. Byron travelled extensively, and his reflections on the great monuments of the classic age provoked a passion for Greek styles in architecture and the decorative arts.

The situation was a gold mine for the newly industrialized manufacturers. They could mass-produce imitations of all the accoutrements necessary for a mediaeval or classical look at prices an average person could afford. For the first time, the working class could aspire to at least a semblance of the trappings of the affluent. To the poor, who had always lived with plain things, rich meant fancy, ornate and elaborate: ostentatious displays of wealth were proof of one's success. For the manufacturer who catered to the mass market, it was just as easy to produce something ornate as something plain, and while the Victorians might tolerate the occasional straight line or absence of ornament, they did not see any special artistic or moral merit in it. So designs became very ornate; it probably made people feel they were getting their money's worth.

Improved communications, literacy and travel whetted the

public appetite for novelty and change. Manufacturers were only too happy to oblige, and for their source of "new" designs, they turned to the past. The Victorians went from one historical source of decorative inspiration to another. They had a go at all the ancient cultures, then produced hybrid styles that borrowed bits from each.

The New World was not immune to Victorian taste. On the true frontiers of settlement, where life was still a struggle for survival and home might be a sod hut or log cabin with furniture made from tree stumps, no one made much attempt to follow the latest fashion in interior decoration. But that changed in 1884, when Eaton's began a nationwide mail-order business that gave even the most remote pioneer farm access to the same merchandise offered in downtown Toronto. Then in 1886, the first transcontinental passenger train reached Vancouver from Montreal, cutting the travel time between the two cities from the months required by

clipper ship to one week, hardly any longer than it takes today. Henceforth, with very little delay, newspapers and magazines would inform North Americans of Paris fashions for the coming season or of the Queen's favourite wallpaper colours, and whether from nostalgia for the old country or from the age-old desire to be at the forefront of fashion, people would do their best to copy the latest trends.

Stencilling was one of the tools at the disposal of the Victorian decorator, and a highly developed one, but in North America, it was not used as much as wallpaper. It is never given special mention in descriptions of interiors; rather, it is treated as simply one more way of applying decoration.

Victorians were very generous in their wall and ceiling decoration, but they always followed well-defined rules. The more important the room, the more elaborate its decoration. Service rooms and maids' quarters made do with plain painted walls, but in other rooms, wall areas were

broken up with a dado or wainscotting on the lower part and a picture rail near the top. The most common treatment for parlours and dining rooms included wainscotting, either panelled or covered in dark wallpaper, a lighter wallpaper above and finally a wide papered frieze at the top. As a general rule, friezes were 9 to 18 inches wide (Montgomery Ward's mail-order catalogue stated that anything narrower than 9 inches would make ceilings look lower). Borders—especially friezes—were often given some visual separation from the rest of the wall: a background of a different colour or parallel lines above and below.

It was common in those days to let a freshly plastered wall dry for several years before applying wallpaper. In the meantime, the wall might be painted with distemper and embellished temporarily with stencilled friezes and dadoes so as to avoid that horror of 19th-century horrors, the blank wall. Another "intermediate" use for stencilling, described in a 1913 manual, *The*

Paper Hanger's Companion, was to help lay out decorations that were finished with freehand painting. Stencils to be used in such a preliminary process could have as many bridges as they needed without much regard for the design, because the gaps were painted out by hand in the finishing stages.

Stencilling was also used as a final decoration in its own right. Motifs were chosen from Gothic, Greek and mediaeval sources, with occasional exotic influences from the Orient. Stencil work varied widely in complexity, but it was, in general, more elegant and ornate than earlier rural styles. Modest cottages without elaborate plasterwork or panelled wainscotting used simple monochromatic borders to create dadoes and friezes at the bases and tops of walls. An ordinary housepainter, or even a homeowner, would be quite capable of doing them.

Richer dwellings used stencil designs that were more elaborate, involved several colours and demanded more skill to apply. The most complex stencil work, fit for the grandest of mansions, would astonish anyone who equates stencilling with ducks and pineapples. It was elaborate, finely executed and grand in scale, without evidence of the bridges that characterize more pedestrian work, and it encompassed a vast range of designs, from simple Greek borders to complex artistic compositions executed by highly skilled artisans.

Wealthy North Americans did not hesitate to import an artist from the old country to embellish their interiors. In Vancouver, my mother's uncle had an impressive house built in the city's West End in the late 1800s. Being of Scottish background and wanting a visual reminder of his origins, he brought an artist from Scotland to paint scenes of the Highlands on all the walls in the large front hall. During the late 1800s, however, mural painting—and stencilling, in particular—were more common in commercial buildings and government offices than in private houses. Nevertheless, they were still relatively inexpensive methods of imparting important-looking decoration to spacious interiors.

I have not said much about colour yet because different schemes characterized different parts of the century. Pastels were popular in the early part of Victoria's reign. Then, as furniture became heavier and more elaborate, room colours became richer and darker, although bedrooms often remained light and cheerful. There was even a brief period in the mid-1800s when very bright colours were fashionable. By the 1870s, the more subdued tertiary hues—slightly muddy versions of reds, greens, browns, blues, pinks and golds—were in favour and remained so for at least two decades. The darkest shades were used in dining rooms. Cream, which had been considered daring, was used in combination with pastels in the 1890s.

THE BEST VICTORIAN STENCILLING WAS ELABORATE, FINELY EXECUTED AND GRAND IN SCALE. PRESERVED EXAMPLES, SUCH AS THE CEILING DETAIL, ABOVE, AND THE GARLAND FRIEZE, LEFT, FROM THE CAPTAIN'S PALACE, A RESTAURANT IN VICTORIA, BRITISH COLUMBIA, BOTH BREATHTAKING IN THEIR COMPLEXITY, COMBINE FORMAL STENCILLING WITH FREEHAND PAINTING. SOME VICTORIAN MOTIFS, FACING PAGE, WERE SIMPLE ENOUGH TO MATCH THE SKILLS OF THOSE JUST BEGINNING TO MASTER STENCILLING TECHNIQUES.

125

MODERN

TIRED OF VICTORIAN EXCESS, TURN-OF-THE-CENTURY ARTISTS URGED A RETURN TO BASIC DESIGN PRINCIPLES, A MOVEMENT THAT BECAME ART NOUVEAU. NOTED FOR ITS CLEAN LINES, FACING PAGE, AND ITS CHECKERBOARD MOTIFS, BELOW, ART NOUVEAU TOOK INSPIRATION MOSTLY FROM NATURE—BIRDS, LEAVES AND FLOWERS—RENDERED IN STYLIZED, OFTEN ELONGATED, FORM. A PHOTOGRAPHY STORE IN VANCOUVER, BRITISH COLUMBIA, LEFT, WAS DECORATED WITH AN ART NOUVEAU FRIEZE FEATURING AN ARBUTUS TREE AND A HAIDA CANOE.

Not everyone appreciated Victoriana, however. As early as the 1850s, some designers rebelled against the ornate styles and shoddy quality of factory manufacture and urged a return to the uncorrupted principles of pure design and the high standards of hand craftsmanship.

By the end of the century, the small rebellion had flowered into an ephemeral movement now generally called art nouveau. Because the movement was so widespread and so varied in its expression, it had many names. In Germany, it was *Jugendstil*; in Italy, *Stile Liberty*; in Austria, *Secessionstil*; and in France, it was known as *Style 1900*, *Style Moderne*, *Style Nouille* or *Style Bouche de Métro*. But no matter what it was called, the different forms of art nouveau had a common ideology. Its supporters wanted to stop copying from the past and create a completely new style, to promote fine craftsmanship with the finest of materials and to strive for integrated and functional design. Stencilling, which had become a finely developed tool in the hands of the Victorians but which was stylistically mired in the past, flourished again with art nouveau.

As a style, art nouveau encompassed many variations, so it is difficult to describe. Very generally, there were two main forms: the "spaghetti" form, characterized by free-flowing, restless and asymmetrical representations of plants and animals; and the "checkerboard" form, with its rectilinear neatness and geometric shapes. Most of the motifs were derived from nature—flowers, birds, leaves and such—and were rendered in stylized, sinuous forms. One of the most overworked symbols was the elongated female figure, willowy and dreamlike, that proliferated on everything from ashtrays to posters.

Stencilling was a finely honed and extensively used tool in the hands of art nouveau decorators, although it is difficult to learn much about their techniques because, more often than not, examples of stencilled decoration are not even described as such; they are presented simply as painted decoration.

Art nouveau designers were big on friezes—either stencilled or wallpapered—that were quite wide and set off from the lower wall by a picture rail. Another type of interior design used vertical panels of stencilled decoration spaced at regular intervals around the wall. Colours were always flat and unshaded. Some designers also stencilled upholstered chairs, bedspreads and wall hangings. From 1895 until a few years before World War I, stencilled wallpapers, including borders and friezes, became very popular, although they were not inexpensive. The best of these hand-printed wallpapers were manufactured by Shand Kydd of England, but many similar stencilled versions were made in Canada as well.

Art nouveau reached the peak of its popularity around 1900, when it was featured at the Paris World Exposition. After that, the style became commercialized, and the appearance of cheap, mass-produced imitations accompanied its decline. It is ironic that an artistic movement that began as an idealistic attempt to free the public from poor quality, mass-produced

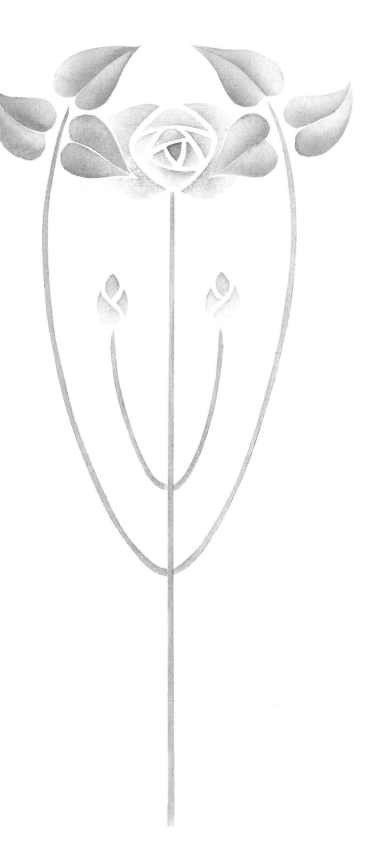

corners of the British Empire and small-town America, art nouveau had little effect on popular styles of decoration. The Victorian interior more or less hung on until World War I, and as it faded away, so did any interest in stencilling as a decorative tool. By then, inexpensive manufactured floor coverings and wallpapers were available through mail-order catalogues to even the most remote settlements. Factory-produced wallpaper was so cheap that repapering was almost an annual event.

Although stencilling was disappearing as a professional decorating technique, it continued to enjoy some popularity as a hobby. Several little guides for the home practitioner began to appear on the market promoting stencilling as a suitable hobby for the thrifty housewife, who could use it to embellish her home and furnishings at little cost. A 1908 manual for the American housewife, entitled *Art & Economy in Home Decoration*, includes instructions on stencilling curtains and walls and assures the reader that "people with no knowledge of drawing have frequently made good stencillers." *A Practical Guide to Stencilling*, published in Scotland in 1913, contains instructions, a catalogue of art nouveau stencils for purchase and several pages of suggested uses for the designs: a collar box, a bag for shaving papers, ink blotters, fireplace drapings—all quaintly characteristic of the time. In Toronto, the December 1910 issue of *The Canadian Bookseller & Stationer* warned merchants not to think that interest in stencilling had died out just because the de-

THE EXQUISITE ART NOUVEAU FRIEZE, ABOVE, AT THE UNIVERSITY OF BRITISH COLUMBIA'S CECIL GREEN PARK, WAS STENCILLED ON FABRIC INSET BETWEEN WOOD MOULDINGS. STENCILLING HAS REGAINED ITS FORMER POPULARITY, RETURNING, FACING PAGE, TO ITS RUSTIC ROOTS AND DRAWING MUCH OF ITS INSPIRATION FROM THE EARLY 19TH CENTURY.

home decoration should itself end in a flurry of cheap, factory-made imitations. In fact, although art nouveau had been intended originally to enlighten the lives of the working class, its insistence on the finest of materials and the finest hand workmanship meant that only the very rich could afford the real thing.

In places out of the mainstream of fashion, such as the far

mand for stencilled goods had declined. The magazine article pointed out that the craft was being taken up as a "domestic pursuit" and that it was well worthwhile to carry stencil material and paints. It even suggested that stores offer instructions on technique.

After World War I, stencilling went into a long period of disuse as a decorating tool in North America. Its current revival, so vigorous and enthusiastic that it seems to be making up for those long years of neglect, began when the American bicentennial awakened public appreciation for historical American decoration. Stencilling gradually became a popular handicraft again, partly because of Adele Bishop's work in modernizing traditional techniques. Reborn, stencilling drew much of its inspiration from a nostalgia for early-19th-century rural styles. As any style attracting public interest will be manipulated and hybridized until, losing almost all resemblance to the original, it achieves maximum market appeal, so has this original folk-art style given rise to what might be called a generic country style: stencilled images of little houses, all shapes and sizes of hearts, ducks, geese, cats, cows and pigs (usually bedecked with ribbons or hats). It's a style I call "cutely country," although a friend of mine insists on calling it "acutely country." "Have you ever," she once asked me with great exasperation, "tried to tie a bow around the neck of a real goose?" Nevertheless, this particular style has enticed hundreds of thousands of people to try their hand at stencilling and has ensured the continued survival of a long-established craft.

CHAPTER SIX

DESIGN GLOSSARY

I told one of my classes that getting hooked on stencilling would change the way they saw things, that they would find themselves looking for patterns everywhere: in shadows on the lawn, light filtering through a flower, leaves underfoot, a wrought-iron gate, the print or texture of a fabric. Nothing would be safe from scrutiny. Everyone looked at me oddly, probably wondering why anyone would want to discuss image perception in a hobby class that was supposed to teach them how to paint teddy bears on a nursery wall. But the following week, several people in the class made a point of telling me I was right, that they did look at the world differently. They could no longer see a flower without imagining various ways of rendering its image with stencils. They were more conscious of patterns around them, and every pattern they saw registered in their brains as a set of cutouts and bridges.

Menu

Speciality Teas
£1.15

Herb Teas
£1.00

Scones with Cream and Berries
£2.45

Assorted Sandwiches
£2.95

Special Today

Camomile Tea & Biscuits
£1.75

133

My own sources of inspiration have been many and varied, some obscure and some very common. Often the resulting designs will recall memories just as effectively as a photograph album. An art nouveau rose reminds me of a cousin who gave me the brooch that suggested the design. A swag stencil was inspired by a label on a bottle of wine that was part of a dinner shared with friends. And so on.

Good sources of motifs, aside from stencil books, include wallpapers, textiles, books on historical ornament, cross-stitch patterns, embroidery, children's books, lace or cutwork, rugs, chinaware, carved decoration, inlaid wood patterns—the list is endless. Start your stencil design by making pencil sketches or by tracing the outline of the object of your inspiration; don't worry about size at first—you can adjust that on a photocopier later.

From this point, there are two approaches to completing the design. The first is to give it a straightforward, honest stencil style, with obvious bridges or ties that contribute to the overall design by indicating its structure. This kind of image will always be more or less stylized. Stained-glass designs can be translated directly into this kind of stencil pattern, with the lead strips creating the bridges. As the 1913 edition of *The Paper Hanger's Companion* says, "In the hands of a good designer, the ties are a source not of weakness but of strength. He makes them increase and complete the effect he wishes to produce."

The second approach is to aim for a more naturalistic image by trying to hide or eliminate the bridges and to make subtle use of shading and colour to give the image shape and structure. This approach always involves many more stencils and very close registration.

The number of stencils you need for any given design will depend on the number of colours, the amount of shading detail and whether you want the bridges to be obvious or not. You need to work all this out on paper by marking up your design with pencil crayons to help you decide which parts of the pattern will go on each stencil unit.

Once you have the basic motifs, you can play around with them to create borders or overall patterns. At this stage, I often cut a temporary stencil of the basic motif, print a dozen copies on paper, then turn the stencil over and print a dozen mirror images. Next, I cut out this collection of prints and start arranging and rearranging them on a large sheet of paper over which I have drawn a rough grid. For an overall pattern, I might start with a fairly static arrangement of one motif per grid, then I try to generate a little movement by reversing alternate motifs or removing every other motif to make a half-drop pattern.

For a border, I might try a straight line of repeats, an undulating wave of repeats or some combination of the motif and its mirror image. Once I am happy with the layout, I tape down all my little paper proofs, put a sheet of tracing paper over them and trace a clean outline of the whole pattern. For a border, I make two copies, then position them in sequence to make sure that the repeats match properly. I may have to make some small changes at the beginning or end of this basic pattern segment to achieve a graceful alignment between repeats.

A few years ago, I started using a computer as an alternative to pencil, ruler, eraser and graph paper in developing some stencil designs. It makes drawing accurate geometric figures child's play. And you can move the shapes around on the screen and combine them in different ways until you find something you like. When you print it out, you have an exact design—complete with repeats and in exactly the size you want—from which to cut the stencil. You do not need a computer to do all this, but if you already have one and if you can get it away from the kids for an hour, it is certainly worthwhile experimenting with it. Not all personal computers can do this sort of graphics work, so if you are thinking of buying one, check it out first (I use a Macintosh and the MacDraw software).

Once you start creating your own stencils, you will not feel inclined to use other people's designs, except perhaps as a starting point, because it is so much fun to invent and use your own. And that, to me, is what stencilling is all about—having a tool that makes it easy and fun to express your creativity. The designs on the following pages are included to stimulate your imagination and to expand your visual vocabulary of stencil motifs.

FRET BORDERS

The fret is an interlocking design of straight line segments, usually with right angles. Although it was used in many cultures, the Greeks used it most extensively and designed a rich series of variations. Fret borders are easy to design, especially if you have graph paper or a computer. Simply fill in a pattern of contiguous squares, then keep repeating. In general, the width of the straight line segments is the same as the distance between them. The Greeks tried to keep the meanderings of the lines continuous, while Egyptians and Oriental designers did not.

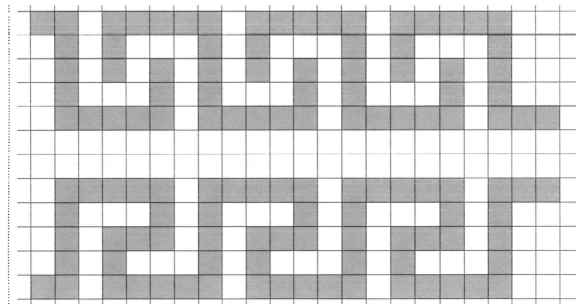

CHAIN BORDERS

Chain borders, as the name suggests, are made up of links of various shapes, presented all in front view or with alternate links in profile. They occur in most styles, but infrequently.

INTERLACED BORDERS

Interlaced borders are lines laced together by passing over and under one another alternately. They are usually symmetrical to the long axis. They are common in Celtic, Arabian and Moorish ornamentation.

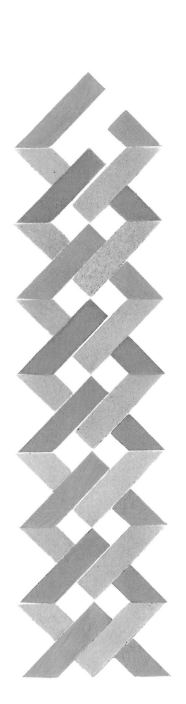

ROSETTE BORDERS

A rosette border is a general name for any border in which the rosette (similar to the front view of a stylized rose) is the main element. These bands are symmetrical and can be directional or not.

LEAF BORDERS

Leaf borders are found in all styles of decoration, with or without flowers or fruit and with various degrees of stylization. Designs are called "vertebrate" when the main stem runs longitudinally along the centre of the band and "undulate" when the main stem oscillates from side to side.

PALMETTE BORDERS

The palmette border, in any of its many variations, is characteristic of Victorian decoration, but originally, it was a Greek ornament. It is made up of an odd number of narrow leaves arranged symmetrically, somewhat like an outspread hand or palm. The centre leaf is the largest; the ones on the sides get smaller toward the bottom.

DIAPER ORNAMENT

Diaper ornament is an interlocking or connected pattern that repeats itself continuously in all directions. The parts do not have to be touching, but unlike powderings, the elements must look as if they are linked.

POWDERED ORNAMENT

Powdered ornament is also an overall pattern that is created with multiple repetitions of a simple motif. It is usually laid out formally with regular spacing but with no direct connections between the elements.

142

143

144

SOURCES

STENCILLING

The Art of Decorative Stencilling, by Adele Bishop and Cile Lord (Penguin Books, 1976).

The Art of Stencilling, by Lyn Le Grice (Clarkson N. Potter, 1987).

Authentic Victorian Stencil Designs, by Carol Belanger Grafton (Dover Publications, 1982).

Carolyn Warrender's Book of Stencilling, by Carolyn Warrender and Tessa Strickland (André Deutsch Ltd., London, 1988).

The Country Diary Book of Stencilling, by Jane Cheshire and Rowena Scott (Webb and Bower Ltd.; Michael Joseph Ltd., 1988).

Decorative Stencils for Interior Design, by Magie M. Maule (Angus & Robertson, Australia, 1991).

Early American Stencils on Walls and Furniture, by Janet Waring (Dover Publications, 1937).

Early American Wall Stencils in Color, by Barbara Marhoefer, Alice Bancroft Fjelstul and

Patricia Brown Shad (E.P. Dutton, 1982).

Early New England Wall Stencils: A Workbook, by Kenneth Jewett (Harmony Books, 1979).

Furniture Decoration Made Easy, by Charles Hallett (Charles T. Branford Co., 1952).

Japanese Stencil Designs, by Andrew W. Tuer (Dover Publications, 1968).

More Early American Stencils in Color, by Alice

Bancroft Fjelstul and Patricia Brown Shad with Barbara Marhoefer (E.P. Dutton, 1986).

The Stencil Book, by Amelia St. George (Stoddart Publishing Co. Ltd., 1988).

The Stenciled House, by Lyn Le Grice (Simon and Schuster, 1988).

Stencilling, by Joanne Malone (Greenhouse, Penguin Books Australia Ltd., 1991).

Stencilling: A Design and Source

Book, edited by Bridget Fraser (Henry Holt, 1987).

Stencilling: Techniques for Interiors, Furniture and Objects, by Jill Visser and Michael Flinn (Macdonald & Co., London, 1988).

Ultimate Stencils, by Althea Wilson (Harmony Books, New York, 1990).

Victorian Stencils for Design and Decoration, by Edmond V. Gillon Jr. (Dover Publications, 1968).

DECORATIVE PAINTING AND ORNAMENT

Authentic Designs from the American Arts and Crafts Movement, edited by Carol Belanger Grafton (Dover Publications, 1988).

Decorative Style, by Kevin McCloud (Simon and Schuster, 1990).

Floorworks, by Akiko Busch (Bantam Books, 1988).

Full-Color Floral Designs in the Art Nouveau Style, by E.A. Seguy (Dover Publications, 1977).

The Grammar of Ornament, by Owen Jones (Studio Editions, 1986; originally published in 1856 by Day and Sons).

Handbook of Ornament, by Franz Sales Meyer (Dover Publications, 1957).

Paint Magic, by Jocasta Innes (Pantheon Books, 1987).

Paintability, by Jocasta Innes (George Weidenfeld & Nicolson Ltd., 1986).

Victorian Patterns and Designs in Full Colour. All 100 plates from "The Practical Decorator and Ornamentist," by G.A. Audsley and M.A. Audsley (Dover Publications, 1988).

HISTORY
American Folk Decoration, by Jean Lipman (Oxford University Press, 1951).

American Victorian, by Lawrence Grow and Dina von Zweck (Harper & Row, 1984).

At Home in Upper Canada, by Jeanne Minhinnick (Clark, Irwin & Company Ltd., 1983).

Interior Decorative Painting in Nova Scotia, by Cora Greenaway (Art Gallery of Nova Scotia, 1986).

Restoring Old Houses, by Nigel Hutchins (Van Nostrand Reinhold, 1980).

A Splendid Harvest: Germanic Folk & Decorative Arts in Canada, by Michael Bird and Terry Kobayashi (Van Nostrand Reinhold, 1981).

Victorian Interior Decoration, by G.C. Winkler and R.W. Moss (H. Holt & Co., 1986).

MATERIALS
Art-supply stores generally carry Mylar, stencil board, cutting knives and mats, various fabric paints, acrylic paint, bronze powders and stencil brushes. They do not always have japan paint.

Hardware and house-paint stores are the best sources for all the miscellaneous needs, such as ordinary paintbrushes, solvents, varnishes, shellac, masking tape, Mactac, vinyl and sandpaper.

Fabric stores that specialize in quilting often carry stencil supplies, especially those used for fabric stencilling.

The Stencil Artisans League Inc. (Box 920190, Norcross, Georgia 30092) is a nonprofit organization that promotes the craft of stencilling. It provides education and certification services, regional chapters and a quarterly magazine and sponsors an annual convention.

You can buy stencils and/or stencil supplies from the following suppliers. Most will fill mail orders, and some offer classes.

CANADA
Buckingham School of Stencilling
205-66th Street
Tsawwassen, British Columbia
V4L 1M7

Ste. 1107-1468 Gulf Road
Point Roberts, Washington 98281

The Cloth Shop
4415 West Tenth Avenue
Vancouver, British Columbia
V6R 2H8

Country Furniture
3097 Granville Street
Vancouver, British Columbia
V6H 3J9

Maiwa Handprints
6-1666 Johnston Street
Granville Island
Vancouver, British Columbia
V6H 3S2

Lee Valley Tools Ltd.
1080 Morrison Drive
Ottawa, Ontario K2H 8K7

Basat House Stencilling
1591 Grousewood Crescent
Kingston, Ontario K7L 5H6

Piety Ridge Primitives
15 Keele Street
King City, Ontario L0G 1K0

UNITED STATES
Stenciler's Emporium Inc.
Box 536
9261 Ravenna Road B7
Twinsburg, Ohio 44087
(The catalogue is expensive but includes products from most of the following manufacturers.)

Adele Bishop
Box 3349
Kinston, North Carolina 28501

Stencil Ease
Box 1127
Old Saybrook, Connecticut 06475

American Traditional Stencils
Bow Street RD 281
Northwood, New Hampshire 03261

Stencilwerks
1723 Tilghman Street
Allentown, Pennsylvania 18104

American Home Stencils Inc.
10007 South 76th Street
Franklin, Wisconsin 53132

The Itinerant Stenciller
11030 173rd Avenue SE
Renton, Washington 98059

Dee-signs Ltd.
Box 490
Rushland, Pennsylvania 18956

Stencil World Inc.
1456 Second Avenue
New York, New York 10021

Peggy Decker Stencils
4281 Melbourne Court
Tucker, Georgia 30084

INDEX

CREDITS

PHOTOGRAPHS

Ernie Sparks: p.7; p.9; p. 12; p. 13; p. 15; p. 16; p. 17; p. 20; p. 22; p. 24; p. 25; p. 26; p. 28; p. 29; p. 31; p. 33; p. 34; p. 37; p. 41; p. 42; p. 46; p. 53; p. 54; p. 56; p. 60; p. 63; p. 64; p. 67; p. 68; p. 70; p. 73; p. 74; p. 76, top; p. 78; p. 81; p. 82; p. 85; p. 86; p. 87; p. 88; p. 90; p. 100; p. 102; p. 111; p. 116; p. 123; p. 128; p. 133. *Robert A. Duis*: p. 10; p. 11; p. 76, bottom. *Renata Deppe*: p. 112; p. 114 (courtesy Art Gallery of Nova Scotia from *Interior Decorative Painting in Nova Scotia*, 1986). *National Gallery of Canada, Ottawa*: p. 115. *City of Vancouver Archives*: p. 126. *Provincial Archives, British Columbia*: p. 120 (*Hollybank, R.P. Rithet Home, Victoria, B.C.*).

BORROWED ITEMS

Country Furniture, Vancouver, B.C.: p. 13, location, all furnishings and accessories; p. 15, bake table, basket, cutting boards; p. 37, table, rug; p. 54, desk, candle; p. 56, desk, dried flowers; p. 60, wooden box; p. 63, pottery, baskets, candle; p. 64, armoire, bench, hat; p. 67, Amish doll; p. 68, all furnishings and accessories; p. 74, table, basket, wooden bowl, wooden tools; p. 81, wood box, pine cupboard, rug; p. 82, rugs; p. 85, rug; p. 90, armoire, bench, bears; p. 102, model boat; p. 133, sideboard, tea set, cake plate, wreath. *Barbara Koroluk*: p. 90, teddy bear quilt. *The Captain's Palace Restaurant, Victoria, B.C.*: p. 111, location; p. 123, locations. *Alumni headquarters, Cecil Green Park, University of British Columbia, Vancouver, B.C.*: p. 128, location. *The Cloth Shop, Vancouver, B.C.*: p. 17, bear and bunnies; p. 85, clown and bunny; p. 88, bunnies; p. 100, lamb. *The Umbrella Shop, Vancouver, B.C.*: p. 25, umbrella. *Byron and Company, Vancouver, B.C.*: p. 29, jewellery, fabric. *Peasantries, Vancouver, B.C.*: p. 41, desk, chair, vase, dried flowers; p. 67, doll furniture; p. 73, framed etching by Jacques Brousseau; p. 100, rocking chair; p. 102, bench. *Edie Hats, Vancouver, B.C.*: p. 53, hats, hatpins, hat stands, undecorated hatboxes. *Form & Function, Vancouver, B.C.*: p. 78, wicker chair; p. 88, wicker chair. *Crash Crippleton's Model Emporium, Vancouver, B.C.*: p. 88, model. *Duthie Books, Vancouver, B.C.*: p. 88, books. *White Dwarf Books, Vancouver, B.C.*: p. 88, books. *The Squire's House, Camden East, Ont.*: p. 116, chair. *The Wonderful Store, Yarker, Ont.*: p. 116, frame.